The Russian Cookbook

The Russian Cookbook

Nina Nicolaieff
and
Nancy Phelan

'Hospitality is still . . . one of the chief virtues of the Russian people.'
– *A Handbook for Travellers in Russia, 1875*

ISBN 0 333 31922 2

First published in 1981 by
PAPERMAC
a division of Macmillan Publishers Limited
London and Basingstoke
Associated companies in Auckland, Dallas, Delhi, Dublin, Hong Kong, Johannesburg Lagos, Manzini, Melbourne, Nairobi, New York, Singapore, Tokyo, Washington and Zaria.

Printed in Great Britain by
REDWOOD BURN LIMITED
Trowbridge and Esher

To
our husbands
Mikhail and Pyotr
and our friends
Pavel and Xenia
who helped by tasting

Contents

Note: Recipes for items followed by an asterisk may be located by consulting the index.

Authors' Note

Emigré Russians have kept the flag of their national cuisine flying in all parts of the world. Even those who cannot remember life in their motherland, or young people born in exile, make the traditional dishes, while the older or more conservative families keep entirely to the Russian kitchen.

This book has been written for those who enjoy or would like to try this cooking. It is possible to produce good Russian meals using local ingredients, continental delicatessen and imported delicacies from the U.S.S.R., available from most good continental food shops.

If there is a Russian food shop — as in most big cities — it is worthwhile visiting it, apart from seeking supplies. Such shops are usually cheerful places, full of Russians talking Russian, exchanging greetings and news, tasting cheeses and home-made chocolates, nibbling hot kotletki and elbowing their way through the ducks, chickens, hams, smoked goose, Russian sausages, smoked fish, black breads and sacks of kasha, the pickled cucumbers, bubliki, vatrushki and piroshki that crowd the small shop.

We have concentrated on typical everyday recipes and all have been made many times by Nina for her family and friends and tested in the best possible way — at the meal table.

Before starting to make any of the dishes, read the whole recipe through carefully.

Where a recipe calls for bread soaked in milk or water and then squeezed out, the quantity is measured in wet bread.

Yeast. Dry yeast means dehydrated yeast, which looks like little grains; compressed or fresh yeast looks like putty and is sold by the cake or ounce.

1 ounce dry yeast equals 4 ounces compressed yeast or 1 cake (American).

Yeast cannot live at temperatures of below 30° or above 90°, which is why most of its rising must be done before it goes into the oven.

Recipes for an item followed by an asterisk thus (*) can be found by consulting the Index at the back of the book.

Introduction

The Russian Spirit

> *'The Russian language has no ascending and descending scale of cordiality . . . only two extremes. If you are not addressed as* brate *(brother) or* galoubchik *(my little pigeon), you are* dourak *or* soukinsine — *terms that I shrink from explaining.'*
>
> Alexandre Dumas: *En Russie.*

Once a Russian, always a Russian, no matter where you live or how long your exile.

There is a vitality in the Russian nature that enables émigrés as well as natives to not only retain their own characteristics against all kinds of influences and persuasions but to Russianise most of those with whom they come in contact. This same vitality, which in the past swallowed up foreigners foolish enough to invade Russia, is, in its more peaceful form equally difficult to resist. Sometimes the victim does not even realise he is being swallowed; he is only aware of being enveloped in a blanket of exuberant hospitality and goes down without a struggle, calling everyone by diminutive names, eating immense meals and drinking vodka like water.

It is not necessary to go to Russia to have this experience. There are émigrés in almost every country of the world (nearly two and a half million Russians outside Russia) and whether they live in Europe, China, South America or Australia they remain fundamentally true to type. Many were born in exile and will die there but except where the blood has been watered down by that of other nations they are still intensely Russian. Even in those of mixed blood the Slav spirit predominates and flares up at the slightest provocation — a party, an argument, a bottle of vodka; while the rest live, think, speak, above all eat Russian, no matter where they may be.

Nina, a White Russian whose recipes make up this book, was

born in Moscow but has now lived twenty years in Australia. Still remembering her years of hunger in her native land, she takes great pleasure in sharing her present prosperity with friends and anyone else who might turn up on her hospitable doorstep.

Every weekend in her white house by the sea the table is spread with her creations; songs and balalaikas vibrate, gaily or mournfully, excited voices argue in Russian, declaim poems or break into song. Sooner or later the Russian soul comes up for discussion, for they talk about their souls as other nationalities talk of the weather, and sometimes people are overcome by it, or vodka, or nostalgia and burst into tears, men as well as women. Then kisses and embraces are exchanged, diminutive names used and over all the noise, the smell of food, the music, the emotion is the warm enveloping spirit of Slav hospitality.

From this hill-top the sea resembles the Chornoe More, and with the ikon in the corner, the smell of mushrooms in sour cream coming from the kitchen, the taste of selodka and dill in the mouth, the Russian language in the ears, it is hard to believe it is not the Black Sea but the Pacific.

Though some of Nina's Russian friends have very little money, their hospitality is animated by the same spirit. When funds are low everyone contributes; but even if there were nothing but a herring and a bottle of home-made vodka the Russian genius could turn it into a party.

To the Russian people, eating and drinking are not just a matter of refuelling or even of creative achievement but a vital expression of the national spirit. Hospitality is part of their nature, their tradition, their way of life. All through Russian literature writers have let themselves go on the subject of food and drink, lovingly, lyrically, realistically; great eaters have always been admired, great hosts revered. We read of a nobleman 'who went through life like a fine old Russian gentleman of the olden time . . . and died of indigestion after a sumptuous dinner at his club.' In the past it was normal custom for wealthy Russians to take the cure each year for their livers.

It has been suggested that this spirit of hospitality derives partly from the Moslem reverence for strangers and came through Asiatic peoples assimilated into the Russian empire; but there are also the facts that Russia is so vast and in the past transport was so bad that people had to travel great distances to see each other. They could only meet infrequently, and so made the most of such occasions. Besides, the winters are so cold that heavy eating and drinking is necessary to keep warm; and Russia is a country that has known great famines. In one twelfth-century famine, conditions were so bad that people ate birch bark, linden leaves, straw and moss, and parents sold their children to foreigners. Even cannibalism was recorded during the thirteenth-century famine in Nijni-Novgorod.

Whatever the cause, Russian hospitality is outstanding.

Russian cuisine

Most Russians, even those who enjoy foreign food, really believe their national cuisine is the best in the world, while the cooking of other countries, if not entirely dismissed or ignored, is regarded with suspicion by the less cosmopolitan. Such prejudices are very high among émigrés, for whom nostalgia and sentiment cloud objective judgement.

Foreigners often think of Russian food as being rich, excessive, exotic. The mixture of races and the country's geographical and climatic differences, added to travellers' tales, descriptions of historic banquets, receptions of Tsars, court favourites and rich noblemen of the past, have all helped build this reputation; yet there are any amount of typical Russian dishes that are neither elaborate nor hard to prepare; and it is certain that the common people, the peasants, saw little of splendour or extravagance.

Even among the nobility lavishness began only in Peter the Great's time — 1672–1725. The early Russian Tsars and boyars ate very simply, though their food might be served on gold and silver dishes. During the Kievan period — the centuries during which Kiev was capital of Russia — bread and meat were the main items of diet. There was beef, mutton, pork, turkey, fowl, duck, geese, cranes, plus the flesh of wild animals and birds such as deer, wild boar, hare, bear, grouse, hazel-hen, etc. Horsemeat was eaten occasionally but only by soldiers or by civilians during famines.

Food was plainly cooked and presented. (Roast meat or ham garnished with gold paper was considered quite exotic.) There were none of the later sophistications such as capons or milk-fed calves or pigs raised on sweet Hungarian wine; no fresh fish brought from other parts of the country. The custom of transporting live fish in tanks was unknown and there were few 'preserve ponds'. Even the Tsar ate only local or salted fish. Fresh peas, beans and cucumbers were eaten in season and salted cucumbers, plums and lemons, though no capers or olives. Desserts were simple — raisins, currants, figs, prunes, pastilla (a fruit-and-honey mixture), apples and pears.

But though plain, food was plentiful. On the Tsar's table there might be up to sixty or seventy dishes — on one occasion 500 — but they were barely tasted and were served purely for etiquette. In fact the ordinary people of Kievan Russia were better fed (and housed), they had more meat and were stronger, healthier and more resistant to disease than the peasants of Imperial Russia.

After Russia's conversion to Christianity in 988 the Church enforced the Old Testament taboos on meat with blood and birds strangled in snares. The flesh of wild animals was declared 'unclean' and forbidden as food. Though the people of Moscow observed these restrictions they were not greatly respected in the country districts. The Church also instituted feasts and proclaimed Wednesday and Friday meatless days; at the same time it encouraged the eating of fish, for those who had access to it. Fish and caviar were very early Russian foods, dating from long before Christianity.

The people also had millet gruel and oatmeal porridge, eggs, dairy products, vegetables and butter. Vegetable oils from flax or hemp seed were used, specially during the long fasts, such as Lent, when animal and dairy products were forbidden.

Bread was always an important part of the diet. In South Russia it was made of wheat flour, in the north usually of rye. In times of famine leaves were added to the flour in an attempt to make it more nourishing.

As well as ordinary bread there was a special loaf, baked with honey and poppy-seeds, for the wealthy and for feast days in monasteries. In *The Life of St Sergius of Radonezh*, who died in 1392, these sweet loaves are described as 'warm and tender . . . and taste exceedingly sweet, as if they had been baked in honey and seed-oil and spices.'

Though all food was kept very clean and out of reach of the dogs or other animals, particular care was taken of bread and drinking water. The early Russians regarded bread (and water) with great reverence, an attitude that is believed to descend from Slavic paganism and ancient harvest festivals. Bread still features in Orthodox Church rites and in traditional domestic customs of blessing and welcome among the people.

The main drinks of the early Russians were mead and kvass, described elsewhere in this book. Wine and vodka were later innovations.

Although Russia has no early literature of cooking, like France, Italy, England and Germany, the old records suggest that meat was either boiled or grilled and vegetables boiled or eaten raw. Corned-beef and cured ham are mentioned but no pirogs (pies), which later became so popular.

Much of Russia's history may be traced in her cuisine — her conquests, assimilated peoples, treaties and alliances, enemy invasions, the legacies of foreigners who came peacefully and by invitation. In the same way, the country's great physical diversity is seen in materials typical of different areas. As Russia lies between East and West her cuisine is a union of these two worlds and of influences that range from Scandinavian Northmen to Tartars, Mongols and other Asiatics.

Certain foods and customs were brought from Scandinavia by the Ruriks, invited to rule Russia in the ninth century; others came from Poland, Finland, Lithuania and adjacent Baltic countries. In the south, as Russia invaded the Caucasus, she adopted Georgian, Uzbek, Armenian, Azerbaijanian dishes such as pilaffs and shaslik. Her wars with Turkey, her contacts with Persia may be seen in identical recipes and names of foods in all three countries — though some of the Turkish words and names are relics of the time of the Tartar invasions. In the Far East, in Siberia, Chinese noodles and dim sims (savoury fillings wrapped in dough and boiled), had become popular.

The Russians learned of tea from the Chinese, of wine from the Greeks — and later again from Peter the Great, who imported French wines. When St Vladimir embraced Christianity for Russia further influences came from Byzantium.

In the great houses it was customary to have a highly-trained chef in charge of the kitchen. Many of these chefs, who were brought from Turkey or Hungary, gradually added touches and recipes from their own countries to the existing cuisine.

From the reign of Peter the Great European influences increased, for this brilliant Tsar imported whatever he admired in other nations or felt would benefit Russia. As a result of his travels in Europe, Prussian officers, Dutch boat-builders, English artisans, Italian and French architects and builders were invited to St Petersburg and with them came Dutch and English dishes, German sausages, schnitzels and sauerkraut, Italian salame, macaroni, ice-cream and pastries, French soups and sauces.

During the period of Anglomania, English dishes were very popular. Catherine the Great, who admired French culture, imported many French customs. Though she herself was no gourmet her grandson, Alexander I, loved French food and in Paris in 1814–15 and at the Congressof Aix-la-Chapelle appointed Antonin Carême, the great French cook, to supervise his table. Carême later went to St Petersburg at the Tsar's invitation. He was also chef in the household of the Russian Princess Bagration.

All these influences have resulted in a rich and varied cuisine of which perhaps only a small portion is really indigenous; yet most of the imported dishes have become completely Russianised by the addition of such typical native ingredients as sour cream, dill, mushrooms and salted cucumber. And of course Russian influence also worked in reverse, to a certain extent. Not only have great Russian dishes become international; Russian names have gone into foreign menus — Orloff, Bagration, Stroganoff, Romanoff, etc.

It is often said that the excessive use of sour cream (smetana) makes all Russian food taste the same; yet there is no doubt that it greatly improves certain dishes, giving a rich bland texture to the other ingredients and being far more digestible than many fats. It has a pleasant mild flavour and a creamy consistency. It is essential in certain recipes and if, as the Russians advise, plenty of vodka is taken with meals, the richness is neutralised.

In some countries sour cream is used as a meat-tenderiser. It is said to soften the toughest meat in 6–24 hours. Its original discovery was probably an accident, due to lack of refrigeration.

Foreign gourmets of the past have spoken harshly of Russian cuisine. Among them was Alexandre Dumas, who spent nine months travelling all over the country in the 1850's; yet though he complained bitterly about the bad cooking he admitted that the raw materials were superb . . . the fish, game, caviar, etc . . . and the spirit of hospitality above reproach.

Apart from accidental discoveries, characteristic features of national or regional dishes in any country result either from the availability — or special excellence or abundance — of local materials, or from prevailing conditions. In the days before refrigeration, when transport in Russia was slow and infrequent, food was smoked, salted or pickled for preservation and to ensure winter supplies. Summer fruits and vegetables were pickled or marinaded for the months when nothing could grow, fish and meat were salted or smoked for the periods when the rivers and lakes were frozen over. Smoked and salted fish, pickled fruit and vegetables are now typical features of Russian cuisine. The flavours that result have proved so agreeable that these measures, originally taken for necessity, are now carried out for reasons of gastronomy rather than preservation.

Russian eating habits

Much has been written of Russian hospitality on the grand scale — of banquets arranged by such nobles as Count Potemkin, favourite of Catherine the Great, with fountains of wine, pyramids of roasted meat and 600 places laid at the table; of an entertainment given to celebrate the birth of Catherine's grandson Alexander, which cost 50,000 roubles and at which the dessert was set out with jewels worth well over a million pounds.

Potemkin, whose lavish tastes helped perpetuate the image of Russian extravagance, ate only the rarest of fruits, the most exquisite of foods. He is said to have bought up a whole greenhouse of cherry-trees, in mid-winter, at a rouble a cherry; to have spent 800 roubles a day on his ordinary table, to have hastened his own death by eating, while in a high fever, a meal of salt pork, beetroots, a goose, three or four fowls, with kvass, mead and wine. By contrast, his royal mistress ate and drank very little and went without meat twice a week.

Such excesses were mainly confined to the upper classes but when occasionally the common people were treated to a banquet they displayed true Russian appetites. At a coronation dinner for subjects, held on the Petrovsky Plains near Moscow, we are told of . . . 'eight miles of tables, covered with white cloths . . . sheep roasted whole and dressed in brilliant scarlet jackets, sausages suspended from poles in rich festoons, pies by the thousand, cakes by the tens of thousands.'

The food disappeared in record time.

Though the nobility used gold and silver dishes and spoons, gold and silver beakers and bowls for drinking, the early Russians had no forks for eating. Each man used his own knife for cutting meat or bread. Peasants used wooden dishes and spoons, pewter beakers and bowls.

In the noble households of Old Russia the family rose before sunrise for prayers. At eleven o'clock the prince would dine with his retainers, advisers and perhaps visiting priests. At noon, all retired for siesta, and supper was at six.

In more recent times meals fell into four — breakfast, lunch, dinner and a late snack in the evening. Breakfast came to be a light meal of breads and tea, with perhaps eggs; lunch, a bout midday, was also light . . . fish or vegetables or pirog (pie); dinner, eaten between three and five o'clock, became the main meal, preceded by zakuski (hors d'oeuvres), and vodka, and including soup and piroshki (little pies), a main course and perhaps a sweet tort. (Most émigrés try to preserve this 3–5 p.m. dinner at weekends, even though they have adopted the custom of their new countries during the week). The evening snack is slight, perhaps taken round the samovar and consisting of cold meats, cheese, bread, sweet preserves or cakes.

These meal-hours still prevail in the U.S.S.R. though to a certain extent modified and adapted to changed conditions, to households where everyone, including the mother, goes out to work, to factories or schools where meals are provided in canteens, to snack-bars, quick-service cafés and the speeded-up tempo of modern life.

But though hours may vary, the fundamentals of Russian meals remain the same. The dinner table is set with two plates for each person, one on the other, the top plate for zakuski, the bottom for the main course. Even if there is no hot course the top plates are removed after the fish zakuski are eaten. The table is set with zakuski, several different breads — black, rye, white — mustard, plain horseradish and horseradish with sour cream, which is milder.

When the guests are seated and zakuski have been passed round, icy-cold vodka is served in small glasses.

Traditionally, the hostess sits at one end of the table, exhorting everyone to eat more and the guests loudly express their approval and admiration of the food. Poultry and meat joints are usually carved in the kitchen and brought in sliced and arranged on a dish. This is a custom viewed with concern by some French chefs and gastronomes. Though they admit its convenience, they complain that it 'tends to destroy the fine art of decorating and dressing . . . and indeed to extinguish with one blow the external appearance of our great French cuisine. . . .'

The Russians feel it is more important that the food should be easily accessible.

Once the drinks are on the table, toasting is constant. This means that all must drink if they are not to appear unfriendly. In theory, with toasts, all approach the same state of intoxication at the same rate but in fact individual temperaments and different amounts of food eaten make considerable and interesting variations.

In most ordinary Russian households only vodka is drunk at meals but in more sophisticated and cosmopolitan families there is also wine. Some Russians regard wine as a soft drink; others believe that it is dangerous stuff and prefer to play safe with vodka.

In 1568, Master George Turbeville, secretary to an English ambassador in Moscow, wrote of the hospitable Russians as —

> Folke fit to be of Bacchus' train, so quaffing is their kind,
> Drinke is their whole desire, the pot is all their pride,
> The sob'rest head doth once a day stand needful of a guide;
> If he to banket bid his friends, he will not shrinke
> On them at dinner to bestow a dozen kinds of drinke. . . .

Despite modern changes and a different way of life, this spirit of hospitality is as strong as it was in the sixteenth century.

Appetisers (Zakuski)

Russian main meals always start with zakuski. Even in the most modest household there is some simple dish, if only a herring, to go with a glass of vodka. The zakuski, which may be hot or cold, become more elaborate and lavish according to the circumstances of the family. If the main course is to be meat, most of the zakuski will be fish, and vice versa.

At an ordinary family meal there may be four or five different zakuski dishes on the table. When there are guests — say six or eight — there could be as many as eight or ten zakuski, and at parties the only limits are what the host can afford and the table hold.

Typical materials for everyday consumption usually include some of the following: selodka (salted herring); boiled potatoes with dill; salted cucumber; smoked fish; radishes; sliced salami-type sausages; ham; sardines; sprats; marinaded fish; liver paste; marinaded mushrooms or cabbage; sauerkraut; hard-boiled eggs.

Strictly speaking, fruit is not used in these appetisers, but there are certain salads containing apple, which, though dishes in their own right, are often eaten as zakuski . . . for instance the Lobster Salad and Vegetable Salad with Poultry included in this book. Some hostesses also serve marinaded fruits on the zakuski table.

Zakuski, which were brought from Scandinavia by the Ruriks, were introduced to France from Russia in the nineteenth century as hors d'oeuvres.

In a country where visitors often came from long distances over bad roads, through snow-storms and other hazards, punctuality was impossible; but guests did not mind waiting for the main meal with appetisers and vodka to sustain them. It has been suggested that these little snacks also helped to slow down the drinking.

Most foreigners have heard or read of Russian hors d'oeuvres;

they have been the subject of many travellers' tales. These accounts vary — from Dumas grimly tasting 'the choicer portion of horse-flesh minced with onion, pepper and salt, and eaten raw as an appetiser', offered by a Kalmuck prince, to Sir Harry Luke nostalgically recalling dinners in Tiflis — which never started till at least two hours after the time the guests had been invited for — preceded by fresh caviar from Baku, bears' hams, mushrooms steeped in wine, smoked river-trout, salmon and tongues. Then into the next room for hot zakuski . . . soup with large game pasties, salmon-trout known as Ishkan — the Armenian word for Prince — kidneys stewed in sour cream and madeira. After all this, to the dining-room for the main meal.

Zakuski can be a great trap. When Melba, the famous soprano, went to supper with the Tsar . . . very hungry after singing at the opera . . . she innocently and eagerly applied herself to the magnificent buffet, which included every kind of hot and cold hors d'oeuvre. She had just reached saturation point when dinner was announced.

This experience, in more modest form, has befallen many unsuspecting foreigners visiting a Russian house for the first time. When you find a table covered with beautiful dishes you naturally assume it to be the main meal. Too late you discover that soup with piroshki and pork fed for weeks on Hungarian wine are waiting in the kitchen till appetites have been suitably stimulated.

The Russians laugh kindly at protests but expect you to go on eating, like the host in Gogol's *Dead Souls*, who rebuked his guest for lack of appetite. . . . One cannot have only one chicken leg on the plate for everything must go in pairs; and it cannot be left at two — it must be three because of the Holy Trinity — and when the guest cries that he has no more room the host reminds him that when His Excellency enters a crowded church a little more room can always be made by moving up. . . .

The only solution for those of poor appetite invited for a Russian meal seems to be several days fasting beforehand.

Fish Zakuski (Ribniye Zakuski)

SALTED HERRING

(*Selodka*)

FOR 6–8 SERVINGS

1 salted herring
1 white onion
oil and vinegar

Selodka is popular at any time of the year. It may be served in many different ways, with garnishes, with eggs, on black bread, with salads and so on; but it is probably best eaten with hot boiled potatoes, well-buttered and sprinkled with dill, chives or spring onions.

To prepare, soak the herring in cold water for 8–10 hours; then cut off the head, slit stomach and clean out intestines. Wash under cold running water. Cut down the centre of the spine, through to the bone and starting at the top, peel the skin away, one side at a time.

Take out the backbone and cut the fish across in half-inch pieces. Arrange it on a long plate, like a whole fish. Put rings of white onion on top and sprinkle with oil and vinegar.

SALTED HERRING IN MUSTARD SAUCE

(*Selodka s Gortchitzei*)

FOR 6–8 SERVINGS

1 salted herring, soaked, cleaned and cut as for Salted Herring
1 tablespoon ready-mixed mustard
3 tablespoons oil
1 white onion

Garniture:

1 hard-boiled egg, chopped
chives or spring onion, chopped

Mix mustard and oil together. Slice the onion into fine rings and mix in lightly with the oil and mustard. Cover and leave for 30 minutes.

Spread the mixture over the herring and leave for 1 hour.

Serve sprinkled with finely-chopped hard-boiled egg and chives or spring onions.

HERRING POTATO SALAD

(*Kartofelni Salat s Selodkoi*)

FOR 6–8 SERVINGS

1 salted herring, soaked, cleaned and cut as for Salted Herring
3 cups sliced cooked potato
½ cup dill-pickle
½ cup chopped hard-boiled egg
½ cup sliced white onion
¼ cup oil
white pepper
salt to taste

Garniture:
1 hard-boiled egg
chives or spring onion

Mix 1 sliced herring fillet with the potatoes, dill-pickles, eggs, onion, oil, pepper and salt, taking care not to break up any of the ingredients.

Pile the mixture in the centre of a plate and arrange around it the second fillet, cut into ½″ pieces, with rings of hard-boiled egg and chives or spring onion.

This salad could also be served on a long dish. When cleaning the herring, keep the head and tail. Arrange salad in the shape of a fish, put head and tail at the ends, decorate top with second fillet cut into ½″ pieces, rings of onion and hard-boiled egg. Sprinkle with chopped chives or spring onion.

MARINATED FRESH FISH IN TOMATO SAUCE

(*Marinovanaya Riba v Tomatnom Souse*)

1½ pound fresh firm-fleshed fish such as snapper, cod, jewfish
salt
½ cup plain flour
1 cup shredded raw carrot (optional)
½ cup oil
1 cup sliced onion
¾ cup tomato sauce
½ cup water

Bone and cut the fish into pieces about 1″ × 2″. Salt them, roll in flour. Heat the oil in a frying-pan and fry the fish till brown. Remove, and keep hot in a saucepan while you fry the onion in the same oil. Fry till light brown.

Add the tomato sauce diluted with ½ cup water and bring to the boil. Pour hot mixture over the fish and simmer for 5–10 minutes. Chill for ¾ hour. Serve cold.

This zakuska, which is very good, is even better if you add 1 cup of shredded raw carrot to the onion and lightly fry them together. The carrot gives a sweet and mellow taste to the fish.

FISH IN ASPIC

(*Zalivnoze iy Ribi*)

FOR 6–8 SERVINGS

1½ *pound–2 pound fresh firm-fleshed fish such as flounder, mackerel, pike, cod, jewfish*
1 *teaspoon salt*
1 *bay leaf*
peppercorns
1 *small onion*
2 *cups water*
1 *tablespoon gelatine*
1 *hard-boiled egg, sliced*

Garniture:
1 *hard-boiled egg*
dill or parsley
Horseradish and Sour Cream Sauce(*)

Scale, clean and wash the fish.

In a saucepan put the salt, bay leaf, peppercorns and onion, with 2 cups of water, and bring to the boil. Add the whole fish and boil for 10–15 minutes. Remove from the heat. Take out the fish, skin it and take the flesh from the bones. Cut it into small pieces.

Strain the fish stock and add the gelatine.

Rinse a 4-cup oval mould with cold water. On the bottom arrange a pattern with 1 sliced hard-boiled egg, then put in the fish and pour the aspic over it slowly. Chill until the liquid is set —approximately 4–5 hours. Unmould, garnish with the second sliced hard-boiled egg and dill or parsley. Serve with horseradish and sour cream sauce.

This recipe may be used for a whole fish. It is also good as a basis for a more elaborate party dish in which a fish-shaped mould is used and decorated.

As in the preparation of any aspic dishes, it will be easier to arrange the decorations if you first pour a little of the liquid aspic into the mould.

Hot and Cold Smoked Fish (Kopchenaya Riba)

In Russian recipes the terms *Hot-smoked fish* and *Cold-smoked fish* refer not to the temperature at which they are eaten but to the manner in which they are smoked. *Hot-smoked fish* are slightly salted, first baked and then smoked at a temperature of 176° Fahrenheit from one to five hours. The fire used is of aromatic wood, such as pine or oak. Hot-smoked fish does not keep as long as cold-smoked fish and should not be stored for more than a day or two without refrigeration.

Cold-smoked fish is salted, then soaked, dried and put into a smoke-chamber at a temperature of 104° Fahrenheit. It will keep much longer, in the same way as smoked ham.

In this book, hot-smoked fish used are eel, taylor and trout; cold-smoked are cod, haddock and salmon.

COLD-SMOKED FISH SALAD
(*Salat iz Kopchenoi Ribi*)
FOR 6 SERVINGS

½ *pound smoked cod or haddock*
2 *tablespoons oil*
1 *tablespoon ready-mixed mustard*
pepper
½ *cup finely-sliced onion*

Garniture:
2 *tomatoes, sliced*
1 *hard-boiled egg, sliced*

Remove skin and bones from the fish and cut into very thin slices. Carefully blend together the oil and mustard, adding the oil gradually as for mayonnaise. Add pepper. Lightly mix together the fish, onion and sauce. Cover and leave for 2–3 hours. Serve in a shallow dish, decorated with sliced tomato and egg.

HOT-SMOKED FISH
(*Kopchenaya Riba*)
FOR 6 SERVINGS

1 *smoked fish, such as trout, about* 1–1½ *pounds*
1 10-*ounce tin asparagus spears*
½ *cup mayonnaise*(*)

Remove skin and bones, and fillet fish. Cut into ½-inch pieces and arrange on a long plate, in the shape of a whole fish. Arrange asparus spears on top and mask with mayonnaise.

SMOKED EEL
(*Kopcheni Ugor*)

Smoked eel	*Lettuce leaves*

Smoked eel, which is bought from delicatessen shops, is rather rich and fat and needs no mayonnaise. Simply take off the skin and remove the backbone, then cut the fish into ½-inch pieces. Arrange on lettuce leaves on a crystal plate.

SMOKED SALMON
(*Kopchenaya Semga*)

Like caviar, smoked salmon is too good to be messed about with. Cut it into paper-thin slices and eat with black bread or buttered toast.

Salted Canadian pink salmon may be eaten the same way.

LOBSTER SALAD WITH VEGETABLES
(*Salat iz Omara s Ovoschami*)

FOR 6–8 SERVINGS

- 1 *cooked lobster, weighing about 2 pounds*
- 3 *hard-boiled eggs — chopped*
- 3 *cups boiled potato, cut into ½-inch dice*
- 1 *cup diced fresh cucumber*
- 1 *cup diced fresh cooking apple*
- 1 *cup cooked, fresh, frozen or tinned green peas*
- 1 *cup asparagus pieces*
- 1 *teaspoon salt*
- *white pepper*
- 1½ *cups mayonnaise*(*)

Garniture:

- *lobster shell*
- 1 *hard-boiled egg*
- *radishes*
- *asparagus*
- *dill or parsley*
- *olive oil for brushing lobster shell*

Take the meat out of the lobster without breaking the shell. Cut into cubes, mix gently with 3 of the eggs, the potato, cucumber, apple, peas and asparagus. Add the salt, pepper and mayonnaise. Pile it all up in a long dish, putting the lobster shell on top and decorating all round with rings of hard-boiled egg, radishes, asparagus, dill or parsley. Brush the shell with olive oil to make it shine.

This makes a good centrepiece for a cold buffet party-table.

LOBSTER, CRAB OR PRAWN WITH MAYONNAISE

(*Omar, Krab z Mayanezom*)

FOR 4–6 SERVINGS

1 cooked lobster
large lettuce leaf
mayonnaise(*)

Clean the meat from the shell, arrange it on a lettuce leaf and cover with mayonnaise, partly or completely, according to taste.

ANCHOVIES ON EGGS

(*Anchovies s Yaitzami*)

eggs, as required
stuffed or filleted anchovies
Garniture:
lettuce
tomato
parsley

Hard-boil as many eggs as you need; cut them into rings and put stuffed or filletted anchovies on each ring. Arrange on a plate, decorated with lettuce, tomato and parsley.

For this zakuska use tinned anchovies already arranged in rings.

FRESH FISH CAVIAR SPREAD

(*Ribnaya Ikra*)

FOR 4 SERVINGS

½ pound fresh soft roe, such as mackerel, herring or shad
¼ cup oil
1 teaspoon salt
1 tablespoon lemon juice or vinegar
pepper

With a fork, remove the skin from the roe, put it into a deep bowl and mix with the fork, picking out all the tissues till the roe is absolutely clean. Add oil, salt, lemon juice or vinegar and pepper. Mix until completely blended and put into a glass dish.

Serve on small pieces of black bread or on rings of hard-boiled egg.

If more salt is added this spread will keep for 2 to 3 weeks in the refrigerator. The roe of any fish may be treated in the same way.

Caviar (Ikra)

Caviar is the most famous of all zakuski. We do not know how or exactly when the Russians began eating it but it is one of their oldest foods. Nor do we know how it came to be called Caviar. Some authorities believe the word is of Tartar origin, others that it comes from the Turkish Khavyah, which is said to derive from the Italian Caviale. The Russians themselves call it Ikra, with the accent on the second syllable.

It soon became appreciated in other countries. The Greeks, who received it through their trade with the present Kuban district, regarded it as a great delicacy; and in Elizabethan England it was so esteemed as to be almost a symbol of exclusiveness. Shakespeare, in *Hamlet*, speaks of 'Caviar to the general', meaning 'above the heads of the crowd'.

The preparation and transportation of caviar are very expensive, which is why it is still a luxury. It is sold either fresh or pressed. The former, which is the greater delicacy, is soft and more perishable than pressed caviar. When pressed it is very black, the eggs are harder and it travels well, which is why it is more often encountered outside Russia than fresh caviar.

There are three grades of black caviar. The best and most expensive is *Beluga*, which is actually pale grey, with large eggs about the size of buckshot; *Sevruga* is also pale grey but the eggs are smaller; and *Ossetrina*, which has quite small eggs, is a darker grey. Experts claim they can tell which area the caviar comes from by its flavour.

These so-called black caviars are the roe of the sturgeon, but there is also a red caviar which comes from the salmon. It has large translucent eggs, like miniature bubbles, orange in colour and very salty. Though cheaper than black it is very good and highly nutritious.

Brillat-Savarin says that caviar 'rouses the instinct of reproduction in either sex'.

Though most of us regard it as a luxury, in Russia compressed caviar is used as army rations because of its highly-concentrated nutritional value and because it keeps for long periods. Russian cooks also use caviar, pounded and diluted with cold water, for clarifying soups; while red caviar is dried and used as fuel by peasants during the salmon breeding season in such areas as the Amur River, where the whole waterway becomes blocked with masses of these orange eggs.

There are two good rules for buying and eating caviar: buy the very best you can afford; and eat it plain, on buttered toast or bread or with blini, (Russian pancakes*). It should always be kept very cold and served in a suitably elegant crystal dish, if possible one which has a pocket for ice.

Egg Zakuski (Yaichniye Zakuski)

SAVOURY EGGS

(*Farsherovaniye Yaitza*)

FOR 6 SERVINGS

6 hard-boiled eggs
2 tablespoons butter
2 tablespoons anchovy paste
3 small tomatoes, sliced
salt and pepper to taste

Cut the eggs in halves. Carefully take out the yolks and blend smoothly with the butter and anchovy paste. Fill the egg-white with this paste, using a teaspoon or better still a pastry or icing tube. Put a ½-slice of tomato on each egg and arrange on a dish.

These savoury eggs may be varied by using herring, caviar, tomato sauce, salmon, fish paste, curry or any other flavour instead of anchovy paste.

EGGS WITH HORSERADISH SAUCE
(*Yaitza s Krhenom*)
FOR 6 SERVINGS

6 hard-boiled eggs
½ cup mayonnaise(*)
½ cup sour cream
1 tablespoon horseradish
salt
pepper

Cut eggs in halves and put into a 2-inch deep glass or crystal dish. Mix the rest of the ingredients together and pour over the eggs about 30 minutes before serving.

GRILLED HALF-EGGS
(*Pechoniye Yaitza*)
FOR 6 SERVINGS

6 large hard-boiled eggs
1 tablespoon butter
2 tablespoons chopped dill
¼ teaspoon salt
pepper

Cut eggs — still in shells — in halves. Remove any small chips. With a teaspoon carefully take out yolks and whites, trying not to break shells. Put eggs in a dish and mash up with a fork. Add butter, dill, salt and pepper. Mix well. Put the mixture back into the shells and grill under a medium heat for 5–10 minutes, watching all the time as they burn easily. Serve hot or cold.

Vegetable Zakuski (Ovoschniye Zakuski)

STUFFED GREEN PEPPERS
(*Farsherovani Peretz*)
FOR 6–8 SERVINGS

4 or 5 medium-sized green peppers
½ cup oil for frying
1 pound new carrots, shredded
½ cup tomato sauce
½ teaspoon salt
pepper
½ cup water

This is a very simple but extremely good zakuska.

Prepare the peppers by cutting off the tops and taking out the seeds. Make the stuffing by frying the onion, then adding the shredded carrots and frying together for a few minutes. Add the tomato sauce, salt and pepper. Put the mixture into the raw peppers, put them into a saucepan with the water and simmer for 20 minutes or until cooked. Serve cold.

Extra peppers could also be cut up into strips, ½-inch by 1 inch, and mixed with the filling; or ½ cup of cooked rice could be added to the stuffing.

POOR MAN'S CAVIAR
(*Baklazhanaya Ikra*)
FOR 6 SERVINGS

1 *medium-sized aubergine*
enough water to cover aubergine
½ *cup chopped onion*
½ *cup vegetable oil*
½ *teaspoon salt*
pepper to taste
¼ *cup tomato sauce*

Cook the aubergine in water for about 15 minutes. Drain it, peel off the skin and chop it very fine.

Fry the onion in oil until golden-brown. Add the aubergine, salt, pepper, tomato sauce. Mix together and simmer for 5–10 minutes. Cool. Put it into a glass dish and serve cold. Excellent on black or white bread.

AUBERGINE WITH VEGETABLES
(*Baklazhan s Ovoshami*)
FOR 6–8 SERVINGS

1 *small aubergine*
½ *cup vegetable oil*
½ *cup chopped onion*
1 *cup finely-diced raw carrots*
1 *cup peeled and chopped fresh tomato*
1 *cup finely-diced vegetable marrow*
½ *teaspoon salt*
pepper to taste
½ *cup water*

Peel the aubergine and cut it into cubes. Fry the onion in oil till light-brown. Add the rest of the ingredients and fry for 5 minutes. Add water and simmer in covered saucepan for 30 minutes. Serve cold.

STEWED VEGETABLES

(*Tushoniye Ovoschi*)

FOR 6–8 SERVINGS

2 large marrow, about 1 pound each
3 medium-sized white onions
½ pound green runner beans
½ pound raw carrots
½ cup oil
pepper
1 teaspoon salt
½ cup water

Garniture:
dill
Chives or spring onions

Peel marrow and onion and cut into rings. Cut the beans into sections, diagonally. Peel and shred the carrots. Arrange all in a casserole in layers, starting with the marrow. Mix together the oil and water. Pour over vegetables. Bring to the boil, then cook for 30–45 minutes on low heat. Allow to cool. Put into a glass dish and sprinkle with dill, chives or spring onions.

This may be served hot or cold. When cold it is used as a zakuska, when hot as a garnish for meat.

VEGETABLE SALAD

(*Vinegret*)

FOR 7–8 SERVINGS

This salad, served without meat and with mayonnaise, is usually called Russian Salad by non-Russians.

For dressing:
½ cup oil
¼ cup vinegar

For salad:
2 cups cooked diced potatoes
1 cup cooked diced beetroot
1 cup cooked diced carrot
½ cup salted cucumber
¼ cup finely-chopped onion
½ cup fresh diced cooking apple
salt
pepper

Alternative dressing:
Sour cream or *mayonnaise*(*)

Garniture:
2 hard-boiled eggs
lettuce leaves

Mix together oil and vinegar, if using this dressing; then put all ingredients into a bowl, add chosen dressing and mix all together carefully, trying not to break up the diced vegetables. Put into a glass dish or plate and arrange lettuce leaves round. Make a daisy pattern on top, using yolk of egg for centre and cutting whites to make 6 or 8 petals. Serve cold.

To make a more substantial dish, add any cold meat, poultry or fish pieces or finely-chopped herring.

POTATO SALAD

(Kartofelni Salat)

FOR 6–8 SERVINGS

3 *cups cold cooked sliced potatoes*
½ *cup sliced white onions*
2 *hard-boiled eggs — chopped*
1 *cup sour cream or mayonnaise*(*)
salt
pepper

Garniture:
dill

Mix all the ingredients together lightly, put into a salad dish and garnish with dill.

SAUERKRAUT

(Kvashenaya Kapusta)

FOR 4 SERVINGS

2 *cups sauerkraut*
¼ *cup vinegar*
¼ *cup vegetable oil*

Garniture:
Spring onion or parsley

Mix well and leave for 10 minutes. Put into a glass dish and decorate with spring onion or parsley.

RADISHES WITH SOUR CREAM

Rediska v Smetane

FOR 4 SERVINGS

2 *cups washed and finely-sliced radishes*
pinch of salt
½ *cup sour cream*

Mix all together but not till 5 minutes before serving, otherwise the radishes will give out juice and make the sour cream watery.

FRESH SPRING SALAD
(*Zeleni Salat*)
FOR 6 SERVINGS

1 *head lettuce*
1 *cucumber*
6–8 *radishes*
dill
spring onions

For dressing:
½ *cup sour cream*
1 *teaspoon sugar*
½ *teaspoon salt*

Garniture:
dill

Wash and cut the lettuce, not too fine. Slice the cucumber and radish in thin half-slices. Chop dill and spring onions. Mix all together.

Combine sour cream, sugar and salt and leave for 3–4 minutes. Just before serving, pour mixture over the salad, mix lightly and sprinkle with dill.

This salad is often used as accompaniment for meat dishes.

Meat Zakuski (Myasniye Zakuski)

TOMATO AND MEAT SALAD
(*Pomidori s Myasom*)
FOR 4 SERVINGS

4 *medium-sized tomatoes*
1 *cup cold cooked pieces of meat (veal, lamb, beef, pork or chicken, or a mixture)*
½ *cup cooked ham*
1 *hard-boiled egg*
¼ *cup mayonnaise*(*)
½ *teaspoon salt*
pepper
3–4 *radishes*

Garniture:
lettuce leaves

Wash tomatoes, cut off tops and with a sharp teaspoon remove the centres. Set empty tomatoes upside-down to drain off juice.

Cut the cold meat and the ham into fine straws, about 1 inch long. With egg-cutter, slice off 4 rings of hard-boiled egg — 1 for each tomato — and chop the rest of the eggs very fine. Mix together meat, ham, chopped egg and mayonnaise. Add salt and pepper to taste. Fill the tomato cases with this mixture and put 1 ring of hard-boiled egg on top of each. Make Radish Roses (see below) and set one on each egg slice. Serve arranged on a plate of lettuce leaves.

For the Radish Roses cut the red skin of the radish in 5 or 6 sections to about half-way down the radish, then gently, with knife point, ease the section of cut skin away till it stands up like a petal. Cut carefully and not too deeply into the radish.

VEAL BRAWN
(Holodetz)

FOR 6–8 SERVINGS

2 shins of veal on the bone
1 onion
2 new peeled carrots
1 bay leaf
1 teaspoon salt
pepper
enough cold water to cover the veal
1 teaspoon gelatine

Garniture:
parsley
radish roses (see above)
½ cup cooked green peas
1 hard-boiled egg

Put the veal with the onion, carrots, bay leaf, salt and pepper into saucepan of cold water, bring to boil and simmer until the meat starts to separate from the bones. Remove the carrots and meat, strain the stock and add the gelatine. Take the meat off the bones and cut into small pieces. Make a pattern with the carrots, cooked peas and rings of hard-boiled egg on the bottom of a 6-cup mould which has been rinsed out with cold water. Put the meat on top and add the stock very carefully, trying not to disturb the pattern. Chill until set, about 4–6 hours, then unmould and garnish with parsley and Radish Roses(*).

This recipe could also be used for pigs' trotters or pigs' head, chicken or goose giblets and hearts, instead of veal shanks.

LIVER PASTE
(*Pashtet*)
FOR 4 SERVINGS

1 pound chicken liver
¼ cup chopped onion
8 tablespoons butter
¼ teaspoon salt
pepper
½ cup cool boiled water or meat stock

Wash and clean the liver of all tissue. Fry the onion lightly in half the butter. Add liver, salt and pepper and fry with onion for 5 minutes, then cover frying-pan and simmer until liver is cooked through. Watch carefully that it does not become too dry. If this happens add ¼ cup water or stock.

Put the mixture through a meat grinder 2 or 3 times, with 4 tablespoons butter. Mix all together. If it seems too dry add a little of the cool water or stock. Pile the liver paste on a plate in a pyramid and garnish with the remaining 4 tablespoons butter, softened, forcing it through an icing tube.

HOME-MADE HAM
(*Vetchina Domashnaya*)

1 leg fresh pork
1½ pounds plain flour
1 teaspoon salt
water

Ask the butcher to pump the leg some hours before you are going to cook it, and hang it to drain for about 2 hours. It is best to order the meat in advance, which gives the butcher time to pump and drain it.

Preheat oven to Reg. 3–4: 350°.

Mix the flour, salt and water to a thick dough. Roll out and wrap round the meat. Bake in a moderate oven for about 30 minutes to the pound. If it is a very young pig, 20 minutes to the pound should be enough.

Take it out of the oven and let it cool; then remove the flour-and-water case, peel the skin back half-way, pin it down with cloves or decorated toothpicks.

This dish is delicious hot. When eating it hot take the dough off when it comes from the oven, brush the skin with butter or fat and put back into the oven to brown.

TONGUE IN ASPIC

(*Zalivnoye iz yazika*)

FOR 8 SERVINGS

1 fresh ox tongue
enough water or stock to cover it
2 peeled raw carrots
1 onion
1 bay leaf
½ teaspoon peppercorns
1 teaspoon salt
2 tablespoons gelatine
1 hard-boiled egg

Garniture
lettuce
Horseradish Sauce(*)

Clean away all the tough parts of the tongue, wash it well, put it in a saucepan and cover with meat stock or water. Add whole peeled carrots, onion, bay leaf, peppercorns and salt. Bring to the boil, then simmer until it is tender, approximately 30 minutes to the pound.

Leave the tongue to cool in the stock, then take it out, skin it and cut into ¼-inch slices or dice. Take out the carrots and cut into rings. Strain the stock, melt 2 tablespoons gelatine in ½ cup of hot water and add to 4 cups of the stock.

Rinse out a 10-inch round mould with cold water. Pour in a little of the aspic. Cut carrot and egg in rings and arrange in a pattern, in this aspic. Allow to set for 10 minutes, then arrange the sliced or diced tongue in a circular pattern, one layer on another until all is used. Pour over the aspic and chill till firm, about 4 hours. Unmould on a large plate, garnish with lettuce and serve with Horseradish Sauce(*).

POT-ROAST IN ASPIC

(*Zalivnoye iz Myasa*)

FOR 8 SERVINGS

The better the beef, the better this dish.

2–3 pounds beef — in one piece
1½ teaspoons salt
pepper
1 tablespoon fat
2 medium-sized onions, chopped
1 bay leaf
2 cups boiling water
1 tablespoon gelatine
½ cup hot water

Garniture
2 hard-boiled eggs
2 cups cooked fresh or tinned green peas
1 cooked carrot — diced
1½ cups packet potato straws
1 tablespoon sour cream

Wash the meat and rub it all over with the salt and pepper, then brown it on all sides in a frying-pan, put it into a saucepan and add the chopped onions and bay leaf. Swill out the frying-pan with 2 cups boiling water and pour over the meat. Bring to the boil, cover then simmer for 2 hours. When cooked it should be very tender but not stringy.

Strain the stock from the saucepan, add some more water to bring it up to 2½ cups again. Allow to cool. Melt the gelatine in ½ cup of hot water. Add to beef liquid. Cut the meat into pieces about the right size for serving. Arrange rings of hard-boiled egg on the bottom of a 6-cup ring-mould that has been rinsed with cold water. Pour a little aspic over them and leave to set for half an hour. Put in the pieces of meat and pour the rest of the aspic over it carefully. Leave to set for 3–4 hours. Unmould, put peas and diced carrots in the centre and potato straws all round. Serve cold.

A spoonful of sour cream on the peas and carrots looks attractive and tastes good.

VEGETABLE SALAD WITH POULTRY

(*Salat s Kuritzei*)

FOR 8–10 SERVINGS

1 *cooked boiling fowl, about* 3 *pounds*
3 *cups diced boiled potatoes*
½ *cup diced cooked carrots*
½ *cup cooked green peas*
½ *cup diced cooking apple*
½ *cup diced fresh cucumbers*
½ *cup chopped hard-boiled egg*
1 *cup mayonnaise*(*)
salt
pepper

Garniture

1 *hard-boiled egg*
a few rings of cucumber and carrot
black olives
lettuce leaves
dill

Cut the fowl into dice, reserving the breast, which is used for garnishing. Mix all the ingredients together very carefully. Put them into a dish or on a flat platter and decorate with egg, cucumber, carrot, olives, lettuce, dill and pieces of fowl breast.

This salad is often known among Russians as *Salat Olivige*.

Hot Zakuski (Goryachiye Zakuski)

CRAB AND RICE CROQUETTES
(*Risoviye Kroketi s Krabom*)

FOR 4 SERVINGS

2 *cups cold Boiled Rice*(*)
1 6-*ounce tin crab meat*
2 *tablespoons butter*
4 *eggs*
½ *teaspoon salt*
½ *cup plain flour*
½ *cup breadcrumbs*
2 *cups oil for deep-frying*

Garniture
Chopped parsley

Put the rice into a mixing bowl, open the tin of crab meat, pour the juice into the rice and put the crab through the mincer. Add minced crab to rice. Add the butter. Separate eggs, and add yolks to rice and crab. Taste for salt. Mix well, then with floured hands roll into small balls — or croquettes — about the size of a ping-pong ball. Lightly beat the egg-whites. Dip the croquettes into the egg-white, then roll in breadcrumbs. When all are ready, heat the oil to 400° (when it smokes slightly) and deep fry for 3–5 minutes, till golden-brown. Arrange on a plate, sprinkle with chopped parsley and serve hot.

FISH FILLETS WITH SOUR CREAM
(*Riba v Smetane*)

FOR 3 SERVINGS

1 *pound best fish fillets such as flounder, cod, pike*
½ *teaspoon salt*
½ *cup plain flour*
½ *cup oil*
½ *cup milk*
1 *cup sour cream*

Wash the fillets and dry them on a cloth. Salt them and roll in flour. Heat oil in frying-pan and fry fillets on both sides till light brown. Remove excess oil. Mix together milk and sour cream. Pour over the fillets, bring to the boil and serve immediately.

CHICKEN LIVERS IN SOUR CREAM

(*Pechonka v Smetane*)

FOR 4 SERVINGS

1 *pound chicken livers*	1 *teaspoon salt*
2 *tablespoons butter*	*pepper*
1 *small onion, finely-chopped*	1 *cup sour cream*

Prepare livers by washing and removing unwanted skin-tissue. Cut each in halves, melt the butter and fry the chopped onion. When light brown, add the livers. Add salt and pepper. Fry for 10–15 minutes but do not let them get dry. Pour in the sour cream, bring to the boil and serve hot.

Some other zakuski suggested:
Beef and Herring in Bread Crust(*), *Cream Cheese with Caraway Seeds*(*), *Stuffed Tomatoes*(*), *Poultry Kotletki*(*), *Fried Pelemeni*(*), *Boiling Fowl Fried in Breadcrumbs*(*), *Marinaded Cabbage*(*), *Marinaded Fruit*(*), *Salted Cucumber*(*), *Fried Mushrooms*(*), *Egg Croquettes*(*)

Soups
(Soupi)

Russia has a variety of soups, a number of them adapted from other countries . . . cream and purée soups from France, cold fruit soups from Germany or Scandinavia, others from the Caucasian countries; but some, such as Sterlet Soup, Schi (*Cabbage Soup*) and Borsch, are essentially Russian.

The hot soup best-known outside Russia is Borsch, but many people do not realise there are a number of varieties. To most non-Russians it is a red liquid made of beetroot and served with sour-cream, for this is the type usually found in restaurants. Though beetroot is always included, all Borsch is not red.

It is made in many different ways with different ingredients — with beef, bacon, frankfurters, duck, vegetables. In winter when fresh vegetables are short it could be made with sauerkraut, brown beans, root-vegetables and mushrooms; in spring with young beetroot leaves instead of cabbage.

To make Borsch properly there should be six or eight people to enjoy it, which usually means a Borsch party. The meal starts with zakuski, then sometimes the soup is drunk and the beef contained in it eaten afterwards with mustard and horseradish, or the meat may be eaten first and the soup drunk separately, as with bouillabaisse.

The zakuski should not be too filling, no potato salads or heavy dishes, though piroshki could be served instead of bread. Since the soup is made with meat and vegetables, zakuski are usually fish . . . herring, eel, sprats with eggs, caviar, perhaps salted cucumber. If bread is served it should be black; if piroshki are eaten they should have meat or cabbage filling.

BORSCH

FOR 8–10 SERVINGS

A few beef bones
A 5-pound piece of fresh beef brisket
1 *clove garlic*
2 *bay leaves*
1 *tablespoon salt*
pepper
enough water to cover meat and bones
1 *onion*
1 *small cabbage*
3 *medium-sized carrots*
1 *small parsnip*
3 *medium-sized raw beetroots*
3 *medium-sized potatoes*
1 *cup tomato purée*
½ *cup sour cream*

Wash the bones and put them into a big saucepan with the meat, garlic, bay leaves, salt and pepper. Cover with water, bring to boil, then simmer for 1 hour.

Meanwhile prepare all the vegetables — peel and chop the onion, cut the cabbage into 1½–2-inch chunks, peel and cut carrots, parsnips and beetroots into thin strips, 2 inches long. Peel and cut potatoes into ½-inch dice.

Take out meat and bones from saucepan and strain the liquid through a fine sieve. Put meat back into liquid, add all the vegetables, except the potatoes. Bring to the boil and simmer for 45 minutes. Add tomato purée and potatoes. Simmer for another 30 minutes. Serve with a teaspoon of sour cream in each plate.

When serving meat separately do not forget to put Horseradish Sauce(*) and mustard on the table.

MOSCOW BORSCH

(*Moskovski Borsch*)

FOR 8–10 SERVINGS

This is the famous red Borsch.

All ingredients as for Borsch(*) *plus*

1 *pound bacon, in one piece*
1 *tablespoon oil or bacon-fat*
1 *extra raw beetroot*
½ *cup sour cream*

Wash the meat and bones, put them into a big saucepan with garlic, bay leaves, salt and pepper. Cover with water, bring to boil and simmer for 1 hour.

Meanwhile prepare vegetables. Peel and chop the onion, cut

the cabbage into 2-inch chunks, peel and cut carrots, parsnip and the 3 medium-sized beetroot into thin strips, 2 inches long. Peel and cut potatoes into ½-inch dice.

When the meat and bones have simmered for 1 hour take them from the saucepan and strain the liquid through a fine sieve. Put the meat back into the saucepan, add the strained broth and the cabbage.

Cut the bacon into ¼-inch dice and fry in oil or bacon-fat for a few minutes. Add the cut up vegetables, all except potato, and fry for 10 minutes with the bacon. Add to the broth, bring to the boil, then simmer for 45–55 minutes. Add tomato purée and diced potatoes and simmer another 20–25 minutes.

Taste carefully for salt, since bacon is salty.

To give the extra deep red colour the additional beetroot is shredded and fried quickly for 5 minutes, then added to the Borsch just before serving. 1 teaspoonful of sour cream is put into each plate.

VEGETARIAN BORSCH

(*Postni Borsch*)

FOR 6 SERVINGS

All vegetables as for Borsch(*)

2 tablespoons oil for frying
6 cups water
1 cup tomato purée
pepper
salt to taste

Peel and chop the onion, cut the cabbage into 2-inch chunks, peel and cut carrots, parsnip and beetroots into thin strips, 2 inches long. Peel and cut potatoes into ½-inch dice.

Lightly fry in oil the onion, carrots, parsnip and beetroots. Put them into a saucepan and cover with 6 cups water. Add the cabbage, potato and tomato purée, pepper and salt. Simmer until the vegetables are soft, about 1 hour.

This is the Borsch served during Lent.

BORSCH, NAVY STYLE

(*Flotski Borsch*)

FOR 8 SERVINGS

1½–2 pounds bacon or ham bones
enough water to cover bones and make a broth
all vegetables as for Borsch(*)
4 *tablespoons butter* or ½ *cup oil for frying*
1 *cup tomato purée*
pepper
salt to taste
1–1½ *pounds frankfurter sausages*
½ *cup sour cream*

Make a broth by putting ham or bacon bones into saucepan, cover with cold water, bring to the boil, turn down the heat and simmer for 45 minutes.

Prepare vegetables. Peel and chop onion, cut cabbage into 2-inch chunks, peel carrots, parsnip, beetroots and potato and cut into slices, not strips.

Fry the vegetables in butter or oil and add to the broth when it is ready and has been strained. Add tomato purée and simmer for 30 minutes. Just before serving cut the frankfurters into 1-inch pieces, fry lightly, add to soup, and boil up for 3 minutes. Serve with or without sour cream.

Taste this soup carefully before adding salt since broth from the bacon or ham bones will already be salty.

KIDNEY AND CUCUMBER SOUP

(*Rassolnik*)

FOR 6 SERVINGS

1 *ox kidney*
water for cooking kidney
1 *teaspoon salt*
2 *peeled carrots*
1 *onion*
1 *peeled parsnip*
6 *cups chicken broth*
pepper
1 *bay leaf*
3–4 *potatoes*
3–4 *small salted cucumbers*(*)
water to cover cucumbers
½ *cup sour cream*
1 *hard-boiled egg*
chopped dill

Some Russians make this soup thick but it is excellent when very light and delicate, which is how Nina makes it.

Wash the kidney thoroughly and put it in cold water. Bring it to the boil and boil for 10 minutes. Drain off the liquid and in fresh water with 1 teaspoon of salt boil it again until tender. Leave it in the water.

Cut the carrots, onion and parsnip into small dice and add to the chicken broth with pepper, bay leaf and extra salt if necessary. Cook over medium heat for 20 minutes. Add diced potatoes and simmer another 20 minutes. Cut salted cucumbers in dice, put in separate saucepan, cover with water and cook on low heat for 10 minutes.

Add cucumbers and liquid to rest of the soup. Take the kidney out of the water and cut in small dice. Add it to the rest of ingredients and bring all to the boil for 5 minutes.

Put the sour cream in a basin, add crushed, hard-boiled egg and mix them together. Before serving, put 1 teaspoon of this mixture into each plate and pour the soup over it. Sprinkle with chopped dill or parsley.

SPRING SOUP OR GREEN SOUP

(*Zelyoni Soup*)

FOR 6 SERVINGS

6 *cups of chicken or beef bouillon*
½ *pound young scraped carrots*
1 *small scraped parsnip*
1 *small onion*
1 *tablespoon butter or margarine*
salt to taste, if bouillon is not already salted
½ *pound young potatoes*
1 *bunch sorrel*
2 *hard-boiled eggs*
½ *cup sour cream*
dill or *parsley*

Bring the bouillon to boiling point. Cut the carrot, parsnip and onion into half-rings. Fry lightly in butter or margarine, add to the boiling bouillon and simmer for 10 minutes. Add the potatoes, cut in dice. Simmer for 15 minutes. Wash the sorrel thoroughly and chop fine. Add to the soup and boil for another 10 minutes.

Serve half a hard-boiled egg with each plate of soup and 1 teaspoon of sour cream. Sprinkle with dill or chopped parsley.

If no sorrel is available, spinach, fresh cooked or tinned (2 cups) could be used.

GEORGIAN SOUP

(*Kavkaski Soup*)

FOR 4–6 SERVINGS

The stock for this Caucasian soup could be made with the raw lamb bones left over after meat has been cut off for Shaslik(*).

- 1½–2 *pounds lamb or mutton shoulder chops*
- 6 *cups stock or water*
- 1 *tablespoon salt*
- *pepper*
- *bay leaf*
- 2 *cloves garlic*
- 2 *peeled carrots*
- 1 *onion*
- 1 *stick celery*
- 1 *small green pepper*
- ½ *hot chilli pepper*
- 2–3 *potatoes*
- 2–3 *peeled tomatoes*
- 1 *cup macaroni*

Put the chops into stock or cold water with salt, pepper, bayleaf and garlic. Bring to the boil, then simmer for about 40 minutes. Strain the bouillon through a sieve, take the meat out and remove the bones.

Dice the carrots, onion, celery, green pepper, chilli pepper and add to the bouillon and boil on low heat for 30 minutes. Put back the meat into the soup. Dice the potatoes, peel and chop the tomatoes and add both, with the macaroni, to the other ingredients. Simmer for a further 30 minutes. Serve with pieces of the meat.

To avoid a greasy soup, trim all the fat from the meat before cooking. If you have time, as a further precaution, let the soup get cold and skim off any fat that forms on the surface before heating up to serve.

SCHI

(*Cabbage Soup*)

FOR 4–6 SERVINGS

'*Schi i kasha pischa nasha*' . . . 'Cabbage soup and *kasha* (buckwheat) is our daily food.'

This is a very old and famous saying, known to thousands of Russian peasants and soldiers. Schi is a very typical Russian soup and frequently figures in national legend and literature. With black bread, it is synonymous with the plainest of living. The seventeenth-century priest Avvakem, languishing in prison, was kept alive on 'a little bread and cabbage soup'.

Though Russians talk enthusiastically and nostalgically about Schi, foreigners are often less impressed. Dumas considered it 'infinitely inferior to anything our poorest farmer would send out to his field workers'; and at its worst it is a thin tasteless concoction. As Nina makes it, however, it is delicious, nutritious, rich and satisfying.

It is made with sauerkraut or with fresh cabbage or with half of each. It may be made with meat stock and served with boiled beef or with pork or on its own. Some people add tomatoes.

½ pound sauerkraut
1 *small cabbage*
1 *onion*
1½ *tablespoons butter or beef fat*
1 *peeled carrot*
6 *cups beef bouillon*
2–3 *potatoes*
½ cup tomato purée or 1 *cup fresh peeled and diced tomatoes*
salt to taste
peppercorns
bay leaf
½ cup sour cream
boiled buckwheat (*Kasha*) (*)

Wash the sauerkraut and cabbage in cold water and drain thoroughly. Chop the onion and fry in the butter or beef fat. Cut the carrot into half-rings and add to onion. Fry lightly. Add the cabbage and sauerkraut, cover saucepan and simmer for 30 minutes, with a little bouillon or water, watching to see it does not burn.

Add the rest of the bouillon. Cook on low heat until the cabbage is tender. Cut the potatoes into ½-inch dice and add, with tomato purée, salt, peppercorns and bay leaf. Taste carefully for salt as there is salt in the sauerkraut. If using fresh cabbage only, use more salt.

Serve, adding 1 teaspoon sour cream to each plate, and if you like it, boiled buckwheat (Kasha) (*).

Fish Soups (Ribniye Soupi)

The most famous of Russia's many fish soups is Sterlet Soup, which in the past was only available to the rich and nobility because of its high price. Dumas wrote rather caustically that this was the only remarkable thing about it; but Russians regarded it as the greatest delicacy and certain restaurants prided themselves on the quality of their Sterlet Soup. One of these was the Troitza Restaurant in Moscow, which was owned by the Troitza Monastery. Its only monastic touch was that though patrons could eat and drink as much as they liked the doors of private rooms must not be shut.

Sterlet, which is young sturgeon, could be replaced by other big white fish. In Russia, stock for fish soups is made from the freshest possible sea or river fish.

FISH SOUP
(*Ukha*)

FOR 6 SERVINGS

2 pounds fresh white fish such as cod, haddock or pike
6 cups water
bay leaf
1 tablespoon salt
1 teaspoon peppercorns
1 peeled raw carrot
1 peeled parsnip
1 onion
2–3 potatoes
dill or *parsley*

Boil the fish in the water with the bay leaf, salt and peppercorns for 8–10 minutes. Drain off the fish stock into another saucepan and add the carrot, parsnip and onion cut in rings, and potatoes cut in dice. Boil for 20 minutes.

Remove all bones and skin from the fish and put it back into the soup. Simmer for a further 5 minutes and serve with dill or chopped parsley on top.

Ukha should be accompanied by *kulibiaka* (Fish Pirog) (*).

FISH SOUP WITH CUCUMBER
(*Solyanka*)

FOR 6–8 SERVINGS

7 cups chicken broth
1 cup diced peeled carrots
1 onion
1 tablespoon salt
pepper
bay leaf
1½ cups diced potatoes
¼ pound pitted green olives
1½ pounds white fish, with bones removed
2 cups boiling water
2 salted cucumbers(*)
2 lemons

Bring the broth to the boil. Add the carrots, onion, salt, pepper and bay leaf. Simmer for 15 minutes. Add potatoes and cook on low heat another 15 minutes. Add olives.

Put fish into separate saucepan. Pour over it 2 cups boiling water and simmer for 5 minutes. Drain off water. Cut fish into pieces 1 by 2 inches, and add to soup. Cut cucumbers into rings or half-rings and add. Bring to the boil and simmer for 3 minutes. Cut 1 lemon in thin rings and serve 1 ring in each plate. The other lemon is cut in sections for squeezing and is served on a separate dish.

Cold Soups (Holodniye Soupi)

These may be sweet or savoury. They are excellent in summer and are served very cold. Since the ingredients are chopped up and kept in the refrigerator till the last minute all preparations could be done early in the day, or the day before, and the kvass(*) or wine which makes the liquid added just before serving.

COLD KVASS SOUP

(*Okroshka*)

FOR 6 SERVINGS

3 *hard-boiled eggs, chopped*
1 *cup boiled diced potatoes*
½ *cup diced radishes*
1 *cup diced fresh cucumber*
1½ *cup diced cold meat — beef, poultry, lamb or ham*
½ *cup chopped spring onions or chives*
1 *teaspoon salt*
2 *sprigs dill*
4 *cups kvass*(*)
2 *tablespoons sour cream*
6 *ice cubes*

Mix together all ingredients except kvass, sour cream, ice-cubes and a little of the dill. Put into refrigerator. five minutes before serving pour cold kvass over the chopped mixture and mix in lightly. In each plate put 1 teaspoon of sour cream, 1 ice cube and a sprinkle of dill.

COLD BEET SOUP
(*Svekolnik*)
FOR 6 SERVINGS

4 medium-sized young raw beetroots, with leaves
½ cup water
1 teaspoon vinegar or *lemon-juice*
½ cup diced cooked carrot
1 cup diced cooked potato
1 cup diced fresh cucumber
2 hard-boiled eggs, chopped
salt and sugar to taste
4 cups kvass(*)
2 tablespoons sour cream
dill

Wash and peel beetroots and cut into straws. Cut the stalks into ½-inch pieces. Put in a saucepan with the water, vinegar or lemon-juice and simmer for 30 minutes.

Wash and shred the beetroots' leaves. Add to the beetroots and simmer for 10 minutes. Chill; then mix in with the carrot, potato, cucumber, eggs, salt and sugar. 5 minutes before serving add the cold kvass. Serve with 1 teaspoon of sour cream and a little dill in each plate.

Cold Sweet Soups (Holodniye Soupi, Sladkiye)

There are a number of these soups made from all kinds of fruits or berries. Some have become so sweetened to the Russian taste that they are almost like puddings, but this may be adjusted by reducing the amount of sugar.

COLD APPLE SOUP
(*Yablochni Soup*)
FOR 6 SERVINGS

3 pounds cooking apples
a few cloves
peel of ¼ lemon
soft breadcrumbs to thicken the soup depending on how thick you want it
1 cup water
½ cup sugar
1 tablespoon raspberry jam
1 teaspoon lemon-juice
1 bottle sweet white wine

Peel, core and slice the apples. Put them in a saucepan with the cloves, lemon-peel, breadcrumbs and 1 cup water, bring to the boil, then simmer till soft. Mash well and add the sugar, jam, lemon-juice and the white wine. Serve very cold.

Dry red wine could be used instead of sweet white, in which case you will need to add an extra ½ cup of sugar.

FRESH BERRY SOUP

(*Yagodni Soup*)

FOR 4 SERVINGS

- 3 *cups fresh berries — raspberries, blackberries, gooseberries or black-currants.* (*Plums could also be used.*)
- 4 *egg yolks*
- ½ *cup sugar*
- 1 *cup fresh cream*
- *extra sugar if the berries are very sour*

Wash and clean the berries and put them through a sieve, mashing them to a pulp. Mix the egg-yolks with the sugar and ⅓ of the mashed-up berries. Put into a double saucepan and heat almost to boiling-point but do not boil. Mix in the rest of the berries.

Whip the cream, pour it into the soup, mix well and serve. May be eaten hot or cold.

Fish
(Riba)

In acountry with as many rivers, lakes and seas as Russia — Baltic, Arctic, White Sea, Black Sea, Caspian Sea, Sea of Azov — fish is naturally an important part of the diet, an importance emphasised by the frequent fasts of the Russian church, during which meat is forbidden.

There is always fish of some kind, for in winter when the lakes and rivers are frozen there are smoked and salted supplies. Many people in the inland areas have probably never tasted fresh sea fish at all.

At the other extreme, in the past, rich noblemen in the north of Russia went to extravagant lengths to obtain freshwater fish. Sterlet, which is found in the Volga and other southern rivers, and which can only live in its native water and at a certain temperature, was transported alive across country for making sterlet soup. (It must be absolutely fresh for this purpose). In the days before railways, special trucks fitted with fish tanks of river water and slow ovens for keeping the right temperature were used to bring the fish to St Petersburg. Guests at dinner-parties could be shown the sterlet, alive and swimming, that they would soon afterwards find in their soup.

Though certain fish are not obtainable outside Russia, Nina does very well with substitutes, using schnapper, jewfish or king-fish instead of sturgeon, and for cooks in Western Europe there is a whole range of suitable fish. Though the flavour is not quite the same the dish is still good.

The Russians like to remind you that since fish spend their lives in liquid they should do the same in death, water being replaced by vodka.

Brillat-Savarin claims that a fish diet stimulates the reproductive system and increases virility. This may help account for the fact that the Russians in general are a strong and virile people.

BAKED FISH WITH EGG
(*Pechonaya Riba s Yaitzami*)
FOR 4 SERVINGS

2 tablespoons butter
1 tablespoon fine breadcrumbs
4 best boneless fillets of fish, such as pike, mullet or white perch
¾ teaspoon salt
6 eggs
½ cup milk
pepper
dill or *parsley*

Preheat oven to Reg. 3–4: 350°.

Butter a shallow oven-proof dish and sprinkle it with fine breadcrumbs. Wash, dry the fish with a clean cloth, salt it and put it in the dish. Put a little butter on top of each fillet and bake in moderate oven until it is almost cooked . . . about 10-15 minutes.

Beat the eggs with the milk. Add the rest of the salt, the pepper, chopped dill or parsley. Pour it over the fish and bake till there is a golden-brown crust on top. Serve immediately.

This recipe may also be cooked in smaller individual oven-proof dishes.

STURGEON À LA RUSSE
(*Sterlyad po Russki*)
FOR 4 SERVINGS

1 salted cucumber(*)
½ cup cold water to cover cucumber
1 onion
1½ tablespoons butter
½ pound mushrooms
1 peeled raw carrot
1 peeled parsnip
a few capers
½ cup tomato sauce
1½ pounds sturgeon, or substitute fish
salt
water to cover fish
1½ pounds cooked potatoes

Garniture
2 lemons
dill or *parsley*

Cut the cucumber into long thin strips. Cook on low heat in a very little water for 5–10 minutes. Slice the onion and fry it in butter and add the roughly cut up mushrooms, the carrot and parsnip cut in straws. Fry all together for 5 minutes, then add capers, tomato sauce and the cooked cucumber. Simmer for 10 minutes. Keep hot.

Cut the sturgeon meat into 4 pieces, put in a saucepan with a little salted water and bring to boil. Simmer until cooked, about

10 minutes. Take the fish out of the water, put it on the serving dish, pour the vegetable mixture over it and surround it with cooked potatoes. On each piece of fish put a section of lemon and sprinkle the whole with chopped dill or parsley.

POACHED FISH, POLONAISE
(*Riba po Polski*)
FOR 4 SERVINGS

2 *pounds whole fish or a section of a big fish such as schnapper, jewfish or cod*
enough cold water to cover fish
1 *teaspoon salt*
6–8 *peppercorns*
2 *bay leaves*
2 *tablespoons butter*
3 *hard-boiled eggs, chopped*
1½ *pounds boiled potatoes*

Garniture
dill
chives

This is a Polish recipe, adopted by the Russians.

Put the fish in a saucepan with water, salt, peppercorns and bay leaves. Bring to the boil, then draw to the side of the heat and keep liquid just trembling till fish is cooked. In another saucepan melt the butter and while still hot mix with the chopped hard-boiled eggs. Take the fish from the water, put it on a warm serving dish, arrange potatoes round it and cover the whole with the egg and butter mixture. Sprinkle with chopped dill and chives.

FISH KOTLET WITH MUSHROOM SAUCE
(*Ribniye Kotletki s Gribnim Sousom*)
FOR 4 SERVINGS

2 *pounds boned fish, such as cod, jewfish or mackerel*
1 *cup torn white bread soaked in milk, then squeezed out*
1 *egg*
1 *teaspoon salt*
pepper
¼ *pound butter*
breadcrumbs
½ *cup oil for frying*

Sauce:
1 *small onion*
1½ *tablespoons butter*
½ *pound mushrooms*
1 *tablespoon flour*
½ *teaspoon salt*
½ *cup milk*
1 *cup sour cream*

Chop or mince fish finely and add the soaked bread, beaten egg, salt and pepper. Take 1 tablespoon of the mixture at a time and roll it into a ball. Insert ½ teaspoon of butter in the middle and flatten the kotlet to ½″ thickness. Roll in breadcrumbs and fry in butter or oil. Keep hot.

To make the sauce, chop the onion and fry it in butter, adding the mushrooms which have been well washed and coarsely chopped. Fry together till the mushrooms are cooked. Sprinkle the flour over them, mix well together and add the salt and the ½ cup of milk. Bring to the boil. Remove from the fire and 5 minutes before serving add the sour cream. The sauce may be served separately or poured over the kotletki.

FISH GRATIN
(*Kokil*)

FOR 4 SERVINGS

2 *pounds boneless fish fillets, such as carp, pike, flounder, schnapper*
1 *teaspoon salt*
½ *cup plain flour*
½ *cup oil*
½ *cup cooked green peas*
½ *cup diced cooked carrot*
1 *cup hard-boiled egg, chopped*
1 *tablespoon capers*
2 *cups white sauce*(*)
2 *tablespoons mature grated cheese, such as Parmesan*

Preheat oven to Reg. 3–4: 350°.

Wash the fish, salt it and roll in flour. Fry in oil, in preheated pan, until light brown. Cool for 5–10 minutes.

Break up the fish, not too small, and put it in an ovenproof dish. On the top of the fish put the peas, carrot and chopped egg. Mix the capers into the white sauce and pour over the fish. Sprinkle grated cheese on top and bake in the oven at 350–400° for 15–20 minutes. (May also be made in individual dishes.)

TRESKA IN WHITE WINE AND RICE
(*Treska v Belom Vine s Risom*)

FOR 4 SERVINGS

2 *pounds fish fillets such as jewfish or bass*
1 *teaspoon salt*
pepper
¼ *pound butter*
1 *large onion*
¼ *cup oil*
3 *cloves garlic*
¼ *cup chopped parsley*
2 *cups boiled rice*
1 *cup dry white wine*

Cut the fish into four servings. Salt and pepper them. Melt the butter in a shallow saucepan and fry the fish, while you chop the onion and fry it in the oil. Remove from the heat, add crushed garlic and chopped parsley. Add this to the rice, mixing in well, and spread over the fish. Pour over the wine, cover and boil on low heat for 10 minutes. Remove cover and simmer for another 5–7 minutes. Serve hot.

SAUTÉED FISH
(*Sote iz Treski*)

FOR 4 SERVINGS

2 pounds fish such as flounder or bream
1 teaspoon salt
pepper
½ cup oil
2 onions
2 tablespoons butter
2 cloves garlic, crushed
1½ cups tomato sauce
20 unstoned black olives
½ cup grated cheese
1 tablespoon chopped parsley

Preheat oven to Reg. 2: 250°. Divide the fish into 8 pieces and salt and pepper them. Heat the oil in the pan and fry fish on both sides. (The fish could be lightly rolled in flour if desired.) Put fish into oven-proof serving dish and keep hot in oven. Slice the onions and fry in the rest of the oil. Add 2 tablespoons of butter. Mix the garlic with the tomato sauce and pour into the onions. Simmer for 3–5 minutes. Arrange the olives round the fish, pour the prepared tomato sauce over fish, sprinkle with cheese, then parsley, and serve 2 pieces per person.

ZAPEKANKA WITH SALTED HERRING
(*Zapekanka s Selodkoi*)

FOR 4 SERVINGS

1 large salted herring
2 eggs
1 onion
2 cups mashed potato
1 cup torn white bread soaked in milk and squeezed out
pepper
1 tablespoon butter
¼ cup breadcrumbs
1 egg
½ cup sour cream
¼ cup chopped parsley

Preheat oven to Reg. 6: 400°. Soak the herring in cold water overnight. Skin and remove all bones. Put through meat mincer or chop very fine. Separate yolks and whites of 2 eggs; chop onion fine. Mix herring with potatoes, bread, onion and egg-yolks. Add pepper. Beat the egg-whites stiff and fold into mixture. Butter and sprinkle with breadcrumbs an oven-proof dish and spread mixture evenly in it, about 2 inches deep. Beat remaining egg and sour cream together and spread over the top. Bake in oven for 20–30 minutes at 400°, until a golden-brown crust forms on top and bottom. Cut in squares, sprinkle with parsley and serve.

FLOUNDER AND SPINACH

(*Kambala s Shpinatom*)

FOR 4 SERVINGS

4 fillets boned flounder
1 teaspoon salt
1 cup dry white wine
2 hard-boiled eggs
2 cups cooked chopped spinach
pepper
1 tablespoon butter
1 cup milk
1½ tablespoons flour
1 teaspoon lemon juice
¼ cup grated cheese

Preheat oven to Reg. 8: 450°. Put the fish into a saucepan, salt it lightly and pour the wine over. Bring to the boil, then turn heat off. Chop eggs and mix with spinach. Add salt and pepper and spread in a buttered oven-proof serving dish. Arrange fish fillets on top. Mix milk with flour. Boil up fish stock — the liquid in which the fish was cooked — and add the milk and flour mixture, stirring all the time. Bring it to the boil, remove from the heat and add the lemon-juice. Pour the sauce over the fish and spinach, sprinkle with cheese and bake in hot oven for 10 minutes.

Meat, Poultry, Game (Myaso, Ptitza i Dich)

Winter is the time for rich ragus and pirogs and dishes with kasha and sour-cream sauce. Much of Russian cuisine is designed to keep out the cold, and arriving at Nina's house on a winter day you find the kitchen full of hot delicious smells of traditional warming-up food. You are always greeted as though you have just driven sixty miles through the snow in an open droshky and urged to build up your appetite with vodka and zakuski. When out-of-doors Anglo-Saxons are bewailing the weather, the Russians say, 'A good *eating* day . . .' rubbing their hands, glancing at the grey sky and streaming windows with satisfaction, hitching their chairs up to the table.

Russians are hearty eaters and often become fat as they get older. Among the simple people this is a matter of pride, an attitude understandable in a country where famine was not unknown.

Meat Dishes (Myasniye Blyuda)

ZRAZI WITH BOILED BUCKWHEAT
(*Zrazi s Kashei*)
FOR 8 SERVINGS

Zrazi are a kind of exuberant Slavic hamburger which originally came from Poland but are very much loved in Russia. For the best results buy good beef and mince it yourself.

For Zrazi:

- 2 *pounds finely minced beef (it must be minced twice)*
- 1 *medium-sized onion, put through mincer with the beef*
- 1 *cup torn white bread, soaked in water and squeezed out*
- 1 *cup water*
- 1½ *teaspoons salt*
- *pepper*

For filling

1½ *cups boiled buckwheat (Kasha)* (*)
1 *cup fried mushrooms*
1 *small onion, chopped and fried*
1 *tablespoon butter*
salt

For frying

2 *tablespoons butter*

For sauce

2 *cups sour cream*

Preheat oven to Reg. 3–4: 350°. Mix zrazi ingredients thoroughly and divide into 8 parts. Roll into balls on floured board.

Mix ingredients for filling together and divide into 8 parts. Cut each ball of meat in half and flatten to about ½″ thickness, like a thin hamburger. Shape the zrazi in the depression of a small plate. The meat must be kept moist, so you will need to keep your hands well-floured to prevent sticking. Put ⅛th of the filling in the centre of one zrazi and cover with another zrazi. Join the sides together with the help of a knife. Form into round flat shape. Repeat this process till all filling and zrazi are used — making 8 zrazi.

Heat the butter in a pan and fry the zrazi on both sides till brown. Put them side by side in a baking-dish or oven-proof dish and bake in a moderate oven for 10 minutes. Pour the sour cream over them and leave in the oven for another 5–10 minutes, till the sauce starts to boil. Take them from the sauce, put on serving dish and pour sauce over. Serve hot.

Pelemeni

Pelemeni probably came from China through the Far Eastern provinces and no doubt descend from Chinese *dim sims*, savoury patties, boiled in stock or water. They are now a typical and greatly-loved Russian dish. They are a meal in themselves, though often served with soup. They are very like the *Gushe Barreh* (Ravioli Soup), sometimes found in Persia, though a different shape.

In the Far East of Russia and in Siberia pelemeni are made in half-moons and are usually eaten with soya sauce, butter, mustard and vinegar. In Central Russia they are made in a half-moon, then curled back and pinched together to look like little shells, and eaten with or without soup, with sour cream, butter, vinegar and mustard.

In Siberia they are made by the hundred and frozen for the hunters, who take bags of them on their trips. Once frozen they will keep for weeks and only need be thrown into boiling water for a few minutes before serving. Siberians believe they taste better after freezing.

During the war, invading foreign soldiers discovered piles of hard-frozen pelemeni in the cellar of an abandoned Russian farmhouse. They laboriously chopped open the bags and finding the meat inside concluded this was a Russian method of storing meat. It was, in fact, only the housewife's supply, kept in case of visitors.

Deep-frozen pelemeni are on the market but though they are less trouble they are never quite as good as home-made. Nina, like many Russian women, still prefers to make her own.

When ready, pelemeni are about 1″–1¼″ in diameter and almost round. When served as a complete meal 30–40 should be allowed for each person. They should not be cut, to prevent losing their juice.

TO MAKE ABOUT 150 PELEMENI

FOR 4 SERVINGS

For filling

1½ pounds finely-minced beef
1 medium-sized minced onion
1 cup water
1½ teaspoons salt
pepper

For dough

3 eggs
2½ cups milk
1 teaspoon salt
1½ pounds flour
7 cups salted water, chicken or beef broth for cooking

Mix together the ingredients for the filling. Make the dough. Beat eggs, milk, salt together in a mixing bowl, then add flour and mix thoroughly with wooden spoon. Tip on to floured board and knead until springy. The dough should spring back when pressed.

Cut off a section of the dough and roll out to the thickness of less than ⅛″. Flour it lightly and cut into circles with a glass about 2″ in diameter.

Put 1 teaspoon of the meat mixture in the centre of each circle, fold in half and pinch the edges firmly together; then fold again bringing together the ends of the semi-circle, pinching them to hold them in place. Put it on the floured board. Repeat till all dough and filling is used up.

If pelemeni are being made in big quantities for deep- freezing they must be laid side by side on the floured board as they are made, not touching each other, nor should they touch in the freezer. Once frozen they can be put into plastic bags and kept for weeks.

Bring the water, chicken or beef bouillon to the boil; drop in the pelemeni, 50–70 at a time. Lightly stir with a wooden spoon to keep them apart but be careful not to break them. Bring to the boil and boil for 3–4 minutes. When they rise to the top they are cooked. Take them out quickly with a perforated spoon and serve on a hot dish immediately.

FRIED PELEMENI
(*Zhariniye Pelemeni*)

Make pelemeni(*), cooking in water or bouillon for only 2–3 minutes, then take out and drain. Heat 1 tablespoon butter in a pan and fry pelemeni till light brown. Serve hot with mustard. May be eaten as a meal or served as a hot zakuska.

Vareniki

These are rather like pelemeni with different fillings which vary in different parts of Russia. There are also Sweet Vareniki(*). Vareniki are always boiled, never fried.

VARENIKI, COUNTRY STYLE

(*Vareniki po Derevienski*)

FOR 4–6 SERVINGS

For filling

1 large onion
1½ tablespoons butter
2 cups mashed potato
½ teaspoon salt
pepper

For dough

dough as for pelemeni(*)
¾ pound bacon slices
2 large onions, chopped
4 cups stock or salted water for boiling

Chop 1 onion finely and fry in butter till light brown, then add to mashed potato, with salt and pepper, mixing well. Roll out the dough, cut it out in circles as for pelemeni, put filling in each circle and fold over. Pinch the edges together to seal them, leaving in half-moon shapes. Put on the floured board while you cut the bacon slices across into small pieces and fry them with 2 chopped onions, till light brown. Pour off excess fat and keep hot.

Boil the stock or salted water and drop in vareniki. Cook as for pelemeni. Take them from the water and put on a serving dish. Spread the fried bacon and onions on top and serve immediately.

CABBAGE ROLLS

(*Golubtzi*)

FOR 4 SERVINGS

Stuffed vegetables and edible leaves, which are also popular in many Middle Eastern countries, probably came to Russia via the Caucasus or through wars with Turkey. In Greece, Turkey and Persia the stuffings are often spiced rice with pine nuts and currants, and yoghurt is eaten as a sauce, but the Caucasians include lamb with rice in their stuffed leaves and serve yoghurt with sour milk mixed with salt, grated garlic or fine sugar and cinnamon. The Russians prefer sour cream.

When making golubtzi choose a cabbage that is not too firm otherwise you will have trouble separating the leaves.

1 medium-sized cabbage
enough boiling water to cover cabbage

For filling

1¼ *pounds finely-minced beef*
1 *cup boiled rice*
½ *cup chopped onion* fried in
1 *tablespoon butter*
1½ *teaspoons salt*
pepper
2 *tablespoons butter for frying*
1 *cup water or beef stock*
1 *cup sour cream*

Cut off outside leaves and remove core of the cabbage head so that the cooking liquid can get to the leaves more easily. Put it upside-down in the saucepan and pour in enough boiling water to fill and cover cabbage. Boil for 10 minutes. Drain off water thoroughly and detach leaves. Trim the thick centre vein so that the leaf will fold over easily.

Mix the filling thoroughly, season it and put 1 or 2 tablespoons — depending on the size of the leaves — on the thicker part of a leaf. Fold in 3 sides, then roll it into a parcel. Repeat process till all leaves are filled.

Heat butter in frying-pan and fry cabbage rolls lightly. Put them in a saucepan and pour 1 cup water or beef stock over them. Cover, bring to the boil, reduce the heat and simmer for 1 hour, till leaves are tender, if necessary adding more liquid. When cooked pour over the sour cream and simmer for another 5 minutes. Serve hot in a deep dish, as a complete course.

BOEUF STROGANOFF

(*Bef Stroganoff*)

FOR 4 SERVINGS

It is said that a certain Count Stroganoff (more likely his cook) while stationed in the north of Siberia, discovered that his beef was frozen so hard it could only be cut into paper-thin strips. Having sliced it this way the cook added sour cream, thus creating one of the world's great dishes.

We are giving here the original simple recipe as used by most Russians but there are numerous variations. In South Russia, tomato paste or purée has been introduced; in France, where the dish was quickly recognised as a masterpiece, white wine is used. Different cooks vary the quantity of butter according to how rich they want to make the dish; and spring onions are often substituted for onions to give a more delicate flavour. Rump steak is quite suitable but fillet is far better.

2 *pounds fillet or rump steak*	1 *teaspoon salt*
1 *medium-sized onion*	*pepper to taste*
1 *tablespoon butter*	½ *cup sour cream*
¾ *pound mushrooms*	

Cut the meat into the thinnest possible strips, about ½″ × 2″. This will be easier if it is frozen almost hard. Chop up the onion, fry it in the butter. Slice the mushrooms, add to the onions and fry until almost cooked. Add the meat, salt and pepper and cook for about 10 minutes for fillet steak or 20 minutes for rump. Pour the sour cream over and bring just to the boil. Put in deep dish and serve immediately.

Boeuf Stroganoff is usually eaten with french-fried potatoes or plain boiled rice. Green vegetables or green salad are also good accompaniments.

MEAT ROLLS

(*Myasniye Roliki*)

FOR 4 SERVINGS

2 *pounds thin-sliced rump or topside steak salt and pepper*	1 *onion, sliced*
	1 *tablespoon butter*
½ *pound sliced bacon*	1 *tablespoon flour*
2 *peeled carrots, sliced lengthways*	1½ *cups stock or water*
1 *peeled parsnip, sliced lengthways*	½ *cup tomato sauce*

Garniture

salted cucumber (*)	*marinaded beetroots* (*)

Pound the meat lightly, until it is about ¼-inch thick, then cut it into pieces about 3″ × 5″. Sprinkle with salt and pepper. On each piece put 1 slice of bacon, 1 slice of carrot, of parsnip, and of onion. Roll up tightly and fasten with a toothpick. Fry in butter till brown, sprinkle with flour and put into a saucepan. Swill out frying-pan with 1 cup of stock or water, pour it over the rolls, add the tomato sauce and the rest of the vegetables not used in the rolls. Simmer, covered, for 1 hour, till tender. Remove toothpicks, put in a deep serving-dish and pour the sauce over. Garnish with salted cucumber and marinaded beetroots.

This dish is usually eaten with boiled rice.

BEEF STEW
(*Gulyash*)
FOR 4 SERVINGS

1½–2 *pounds beef steak*
1 *tablespoon butter or other fat for frying*
1–2 *cups bouillon or water*
1 *cup tomato purée*
Garniture
dill or *parsley*
1 *bay leaf*
1½ *teaspoons salt*
pepper
1 *cup chopped onion*
1 *tablespoon fat or butter*

Cut the meat into 1″ dice and fry it until light brown. Pour the hot bouillon or water over it and add half the cup of tomato purée, the bay leaf, salt and pepper. Simmer for 1–1½ hours.

Fry the onion in butter or fat and add the rest of the tomato purée, with more bouillon if needed. Add to meat and simmer again for 15 minutes. Serve with boiled potatoes sprinkled with dill or parsley.

This recipe may be used for pork, with lard instead of butter for frying, and half the quantity of tomato purée. Simply fry the pork and onions together, sprinkle with flour, then add the rest of the ingredients and cook till tender.

POT ROAST WITH MACARONI
(*Tushonoye Myaso s Macaronami*)
FOR 6 SERVINGS

2–2½ *pounds topside or rump steak in one piece*
salt
pepper
1 *tablespoon fat or butter for frying*
2 *cups hot water*
2 *medium-sized onions*
2 *bay leaves*
½ *teaspoon peppercorns*
½ *cup fresh or sour cream*
¾ *pound macaroni*
1 *tablespoon salt*
6 *cups boiling water*
1 *tablespoon butter*

Rub the salt and pepper into the meat and fry in butter or fat till brown all over. Put it into a saucepan, swill out the frying-pan with 2 cups hot water and pour over the meat. Coarsely chop the onions, and add to the meat with bay leaves and peppercorns. Cook on low heat for 1–1½ hours. The meat must be tender but not over-cooked. Add sour cream to the gravy. Put the macaroni into 8 cups fast-boiling salted water, bring to boil again, turn down heat and boil on low heat till tender, about 15 minutes. Strain off water and add butter to macaroni. Cut the meat into slices, arrange on a dish and garnish with the macaroni. Serve immediately.

This pot roast is very good cold.

Kotletki

Russians love kotletki almost as much as pelemeni and salted cucumbers, and eat them constantly. They are extremely good and very easy for a snack, being made of minced meat like fine hamburgers. They are no relation to the French côtelette or English cutlet.

PORK KOTLETKI
(*Kotletki iz Svinini*)

FOR 6 SERVINGS

2 *pounds finely-minced pork, without too much fat*
1 *cup torn white bread soaked in water and squeezed out*
1 *egg*
1 *cup water*
1½ *teaspoons salt*
pepper
1 *cup breadcrumbs*
2 *tablespoons butter*

Put all the ingredients, except the breadcrumbs and butter, into a basin and mix them thoroughly with a wooden spoon. Form into oblong-shaped cakes, using about 1 heaped tablespoon of mixture for each.

Roll them in breadcrumbs, flatten them with the blade of a knife to about ½″ thickness and fry in butter for 10–15 minutes, until the meat is cooked. Serve with boiled buckwheat (*) or french-fried or mashed potatoes and green vegetables.

BEEF KOTLETKI

(*Kotletki iz Govyadini*)

FOR 6 SERVINGS

2 pounds finely-minced beef
1 cup torn, soaked and squeezed out white bread
1 egg
1 cup water
½ teaspoon salt
pepper
1 cup breadcrumbs
2 tablespoons butter
1 tablespoon flour
1 cup water

Mix together the beef, bread, egg, water, salt and pepper. Form into kotletki, roll in breadcrumbs and fry in butter. Keep hot and make sauce by adding the flour to the butter and juice in the pan.

Brown the mixture, then add 1 cup of water, stirring continually. Serve the sauce in a sauce-boat, not poured over the kotletki. This dish is usually accompanied by mashed potato, boiled carrots and salted cucumber (*).

STEWED LAMB WITH CABBAGE

(*Tushonka*)

FOR 4 SERVINGS

2 pounds lamb leg chops
1 teaspoon salt
2 tablespoons butter
1 small cabbage
½ cup chopped onion
Garniture
dill or *parsley*
½ pound sauerkraut
pepper
1 bay leaf
1 cup hot water

Wash and remove the fat from the meat and cut the meat into 1 inch dice. Salt them and brown in butter. Put in a casserole or saucepan.

Shred the cabbage into ½″ strips. Fry the onion, add the cabbage and fry lightly together. Add the sauerkraut, pepper, bay leaf and hot water. Mix all in with the meat and bring to the boil. Simmer for 1½ hours, until meat is tender. Arrange in a deep dish, garnish with dill or parsley, and serve with boiled potatoes.

The same recipe may be used with pork instead of lamb.

STEWED CABBAGE WITH BACON AND FRANKFURTERS

(*Tuschonka s Sosiskami*)

FOR 4 SERVINGS

1 small cabbage
½ cup chopped onions
2 tablespoons butter
½ teaspoon salt
pepper
1 bay leaf
1 cup hot water
½ pound bacon
1 pound frankfurter sausages

Garniture
dill or *parsley*

Shred the cabbage into ½″ strips and fry it with the chopped onions in butter. Add the salt, pepper, bay leaf and hot water, bring to boil and simmer for 1 hour. Cut the bacon and frankfurters into small pieces and fry lightly. Add to the cabbage and cook for another half-hour. Serve with boiled potatoes sprinkled with dill or parsley.

TONGUE WITH VEGETABLES

(*Yazik s Ovoschami*)

FOR 6 SERVINGS

2 pounds fresh tongue — sheep, ox or pork
enough salted water to cover tongue
½ pound bacon
1 cup carrots, in ½″ dice
1 cup swede or turnip, in ½″ dice
1 cup chopped cabbage or brussels sprouts
1 cup chopped onion
½ cup chopped parsley
1 teaspoon salt
pepper
1 bay leaf
1½ cups bouillon
1½ cups diced potatoes
2½ cups white sauce (*)

Garniture
dill or *parsley*

Put the tongue into a saucepan, cover with cold salted water and bring to the boil. Reduce the heat and simmer until tender. When cool, take off the skin and cut the tongue into 1″ dice. Cut up the bacon and mix together bacon, tongue and all the vegetables except the potato. Add the salt, pepper and bay leaf. Add the bouillon, bring to the boil and simmer for 20 minutes. Add potatoes and simmer until well done, about another 15 minutes.

Add the white sauce. Stir it in gently, bring to the boil, and remove from heat. Serve in a deep dish, sprinkled with parsley or dill.

TONGUE IN BREADCRUMBS
(*Yazik v Suharyach*)
FOR 3 SERVINGS

1 ox tongue
enough salted water to cover tongue
1 egg
1 cup breadcrumbs
2 tablespoons butter

Put the tongue in a saucepan of cold salted water, bring to the boil, reduce heat and simmer until tender. Cool it and remove the skin. Cut it in slices ½″ thick. Just before serving dip slices in beaten egg, roll in breadcrumbs and quickly fry in hot butter.

Meat or Vegetable Rolls (Ruleti)

These are rolls of minced meat or mashed potato, with various fillings.

MEAT ROLL WITH VEGETABLES
(*Myasnoi Rulet s Ovoschami*)
FOR 6 SERVINGS

For the roll
2 pounds beef that has been minced twice
1 medium-sized minced onion
1 cup torn white bread, soaked and squeezed out
1 cup water
1½ teaspoons salt
pepper

For filling
1 cup diced cooked carrot
½ pound cooked green peas
1 medium-sized onion, chopped and fried
butter to grease pan
1 egg
¼ cup breadcrumbs

For gravy
1 tablespoon flour
½ cup water

Preheat oven to Reg. 3–4: 350°. Mix together the beef, minced onion, bread, water, salt and pepper. Spread out, about ¾″ thick, on a wet cloth or sheet of plastic.

Arrange the cooked vegetables for the filling down the centre of the meat. Carefully fold the meat over them to make a roll, joining the edges together. Gently slide it from the cloth or plastic sheet into a buttered baking-dish with the joined side underneath. Smear the top with beaten egg, sprinkle with breadcrumbs and bake in a moderate oven for 1–1½ hours. Put on a serving dish and keep warm. Make a gravy by thickening the pan juice with the flour mixed with water. Bring to the boil, stirring all the time. Serve gravy separately. This dish is usually eaten with mashed or french-fried potatoes, which could be arranged along one side of the roll.

MEAT ROLL WITH BOILED BUCKWHEAT AND MUSHROOMS

(*Myasnoi Rulet s Kashei i Gribami*)

FOR 6 SERVINGS

For the Roll: *as listed for Meat Roll with Vegetables* (*).

For filling

1 small chopped onion
½ pound sliced mushrooms
1 tablespoon butter
1½ cups kasha or boiled buckwheat (*)
½ teaspoon salt

For sauce

1 cup sour cream

Preheat oven to Reg. 3–4: 350°. Mix the ingredients for the roll together and spread on a wet cloth or plastic sheet.

To make the filling, fry onion and mushrooms in butter, add to boiled buckwheat, with salt to taste, and arrange mixture down the centre of the meat. Fold meat over to make a roll, slide from cloth or plastic sheet into a well-buttered baking-dish, joined side down, and bake in a moderate oven, for 1–1½ hours. Pour the sour cream over and serve as a complete course with boiled carrots or peas.

ALTERNATIVE FILLINGS FOR MEAT ROLL

EGG AND GREEN ONION FILLING
(*Yaitza s Lukom*)

6 hard-boiled eggs
1 bunch spring onions, chopped
¼ teaspoon salt
pepper

Make the roll as for Meat Roll with Vegetables(*). Chop up the eggs and mix with onions. Add salt and pepper. Arrange down the centre of the roll, seal and bake.

MUSHROOM AND ONION FILLING
(*Myasnoi Rulet s Gribami i Lukom*)

1 large onion
1½ pound mushrooms
¼ teaspoon salt
pepper
1 tablespoon butter

Chop up onion and mushrooms, add salt and pepper and fry in butter. Arrange down centre of roll, seal and bake.

MASHED POTATO ROLL WITH MEAT FILLING
(*Kartofelni Rulet s Myasom*)

FOR 4 SERVINGS

1½ pounds potatoes
2 teaspoons salt
3 tablespoons butter
½ cup milk
¾ cup flour
2 eggs

For filling
½ cup chopped onion
1 pound finely-minced meat
pepper
fine breadcrumbs

Preheat oven to Reg. 3–4: 350°. Peel, boil and drain the potatoes. Mash them well, adding 1 teaspoon salt, 1½ tablespoons butter and the milk. Soften butter and heat milk before adding. (An electric mixer or blender makes excellent smooth mashed potato.) Cool for 5–10 minutes, then add ½ cup flour and the beaten eggs, reserving a little of the egg for later.

Fry the onion in butter, add the meat and 1 teaspoon salt and the pepper. When almost cooked sprinkle in 1 tablespoon flour, stirring continually. Cool for a few minutes.

On a well-floured board or cloth, spread out the mashed potato mixture, making it about ½″ thick. Spread the cooked meat filling over one half, to about an inch from the edge. Fold over the other half and join the edges. Slide on to a buttered baking-dish, form it into the shape of a loaf, smear with beaten egg and sprinkle with breadcrumbs. Bake in a moderate oven for 30 minutes, until golden-brown, basting occasionally with butter. Serve with carrots and peas in White Sauce (*).

As with Meat Rolls the fillings could be varied; for instance:

EGG AND MUSHROOM FILLING

1 tablespoon butter
½ pound sliced mushrooms
1 chopped onion
3–4 chopped hard-boiled eggs
For sauce
1 cup sour cream

Melt the butter in frying pan, add mushrooms and onion and fry together till soft. Mix well with eggs, spread on mashed potato which you have spread out on floured board or cloth. Roll up and bake as for Mashed Potato Roll with Meat Filling. When browned, pour 1 cup sour cream over and leave in oven a few minutes longer.

MEAT AND VEGETABLE STEW
(*Azu*)
FOR 6 SERVINGS

1½ pounds topside or rump steak
½ teaspoon salt
pepper
2 tablespoons fat or butter
2 medium-sized onions
1½ cups bouillon or hot water
½ cup tomato sauce
2 tomatoes
1 tablespoon flour
1 salted cucumber(*)
2–3 cloves garlic
1½ pounds potatoes, french-fried

Cut the meat into ½″ strips, add salt and pepper and fry till light brown. Chop onions, add to meat and fry lightly. Add 1 cup bouillon or hot water, tomato sauce, tomatoes, skinned and coarsely chopped. Simmer, covered, till the meat is tender, about 30 minutes.

Drain meat-juice into another saucepan, add ½ cup bouillon, thicken carefully with the flour and bring to the boil. Add the cucumber cut in rings and the garlic, which you have crushed.

Put the potatoes, which should be crisp and dry, on the meat, pour the sauce over and simmer for 5–10 minutes. Serve as a complete course with buttered boiled vegetables or Marinaded Beetroots (*).

BEEF AND HERRING
(*Forshmak*)

FOR 4 SERVINGS

1½ *pounds boiled beef*
1 *salted herring, skinned and boned*
1½ *cups boiled potatoes*
1 *medium onion*
½ *cup sour cream*
2 *eggs*
salt to taste
pepper
1 *tablespoon butter*
1 *tablespoon breadcrumbs*
1 *tablespoon grated cheese*

Preheat oven to Reg. 3–4: 350°. Put the meat, herring, potatoes and onion through the mincer. Mix them together thoroughly; add the sour cream, all but 1 tablespoonful. Separate the egg yolks and whites and add the yolks, with the salt and pepper to the meat mixture. Mix again. Beat whites of eggs till stiff and fold in carefully.

Butter small individual oven-proof dishes, or one large dish. Spoon in the mixture, sprinkle with breadcrumbs and cheese and bake in a moderate oven 350°–400°, for approximately 15 minutes, until Forshmak is heated through. Pour 1 tablespoon sour cream over the top and serve hot.

A popular and typical variation of this dish is Beef and Herring in Bread Crust (*Forshmak v Kalache*). It is traditionally made in a large horseshoe loaf (Kalach) but a long French loaf could be used instead.

Take out the centre of the loaf, sprinkle the cleaned-out crust with milk and fill it with the Beef and Herring mixture.

Brush crust with melted butter, sprinkle with grated cheese and bake in a moderate oven, 350°–400°, for 10 minutes.

If this is served as a hot zakuska it should be cut in slices before it is brought to the table. If it is eaten as a separate course it should be accompanied to the table by a White Sauce (*). When cold it is excellent picnic food.

STEW
(*Ragu*)
FOR 6 SERVINGS

Ragu is very popular in all Russian households. There are about twelve variations, using lamb, pork, ox-tail, hare or rabbit, chicken, veal, giblets, tongue, etc. All kinds of vegetables may be included and it may be served with different garnishes.

This recipe for Ragu of Tongue may also be used for lamb, pork, ox-tail, veal or rabbit. (If ox-tail is used it should be soaked in cold water for at least 2 hours before cooking.)

1½–2 *pounds tongue*
1 *onion*
2 *peeled carrots*
1 *peeled swede or turnip*
1 *peeled parsnip*
3 *potatoes*
3 *tablespoons fat or butter*
1 *teaspoon salt*
pepper
1 *bay leaf*
½ *cup tomato sauce*
1 *cup bouillon*

Garniture
dill or *parsley*

Cover the tongue with cold water and simmer until tender, then cool, peel off the skin and cut meat into dice.

Peel, wash and dice all the vegetables and fry them lightly. Put them into a casserole with the tongue, then salt, pepper and bay leaf, tomato sauce and bouillon. Simmer, covered, for 30–35 minutes, until all vegetables are cooked. Serve in a deep dish sprinkled with dill or parsley.

PORK FILLETS WITH APPLE
(*Sviniye Odbivniye s Yablokami*)
FOR 3 SERVINGS

1½ *pounds pork tenderloin or chops*
½ *teaspoon salt*
1 *tablespoon lard or fat*
1 *large onion*
3 *large cooking apples*
½ *cup stock or water*

Remove all sinews and unwanted fat from the meat, pound it lightly, salt it and fry in fat on both sides. Slice the onion, add and fry together. Peel and slice the apples. When onions are light brown add the apples and stock or water. Cover and simmer for 15 minutes. Serve with boiled rice (*) or potatoes.

SUCKING PIG WITH BOILED BUCKWHEAT

(*Porosyonok s Kashei*)

FOR 10–12 SERVINGS

1 *sucking pig weighing* 8–10 *pounds*
1 *tablespoon salt*
1 *cup sour cream*
8 *small cooking apples*
a little water
½ *cup melted lard*
1 *pound boiled buckwheat* (*)
4 *hard-boiled eggs*
horseradish sauce (*)

Preheat oven to Reg. 3–4: 350°. Rub the pig with salt, inside and out; smear all over with sour cream. Fill with apples, whole or halved. Put the pig in the baking-dish, belly down, with a little water and some lard. Bake in a moderate oven. Every 15–20 minutes smear it with fresh melted lard. Do not use the pan-juice for basting. If the pig's back is browning too fast cover it with brown paper or foil until sides are the same colour. Test to see if it is done by piercing the thickest part of the back leg. If the meat juice is not red the meat is cooked. The average time is 1½–2 hours.

When cooked, move pig to another pan and keep hot. Put the boiled buckwheat into the baking-dish you used for the pig and mix it in with the meat juice. Chop up 2 of the hard-boiled eggs and add to buckwheat. Put the buckwheat on a large dish, lay the sucking pig on it, and decorate with some of the cooked apples and the remaining 2 hard-boiled eggs cut in long sections.

If you prefer, the pig could be carved in the kitchen and arranged on the buckwheat before coming to the table. The horseradish sauce is served separately.

If this dish is too rich, pour off some of the fat before putting the buckwheat into the baking-dish.

HAM COOKED IN BEER

(*Buzhenina*)

FOR 8 SERVINGS

This is a very ancient Russian recipe, often mentioned in the accounts of early travellers and still popular.

1 *teaspoon salt*
4–5 *pounds of the centre part of a leg of pork*
¼ *pound bacon or ham fat, cut into strips*
1 *tablespoon fat for cooking*
1½ *cups beer*

Preheat oven to Reg. 6: 400°. Salt the meat all over. With a long sharp knife pierce it through in several places and insert the strips of bacon or ham fat. Put the meat with the fat into a baking-dish. Put into the heated oven and when it starts to roast pour half the beer over it. Repeat with the rest of the beer in 30 minutes. Baste with combined beer and pan-juice every 15–20 minutes. Bake for 1½ hours in oven. Serve with stewed cabbage and boiled potatoes.

VEAL STEAK WITH PORK FILLING

(*Schnitzel so Svinim Farshom*)

FOR 4 SERVINGS

4 *veal steaks cut from the leg, about* 6″ × 6″ *and* ½″ *thick*
½ *teaspoon salt*
pepper

For filling

1 *pound lean pork*
¼ *pound ham*
½ *pound button mushrooms*
3 *tablespoons butter*
½ *teaspoon nutmeg*
½ *cup milk*
½ *teaspoon salt*

For sauce

½ *cup chopped onion*
½ *cup tomato purée*
1 *cup water*

Pound the steaks lightly and sprinkle with salt and pepper. Mince the pork, chop the ham fine; slice the mushrooms and fry them in butter. Mix together all ingredients for filling. Divide into four and put one part in the centre of each veal fillet, arranging filling lengthways. Roll the veal round the filling and secure in two or three places with thin string or toothpicks. Heat butter in the frying pan and fry the veal rolls, browning them all over; then put them in another saucepan side by side in a row. Fry the onion in the rest of the butter, and add the tomato purée and water. Bring to the boil and pour over the rolls. Cover, and simmer for 30 minutes. Arrange the rolls on a long dish and either pour the sauce over them or serve separately.

This dish looks and tastes good with grilled tomato-halves, green beans and boiled rice.

Poultry (Ptitza)

PREPARATION OF POULTRY AND GAME
FOR CHICKEN À LA KIEV AND KOTLETS

To fillet chicken, turkey, duck, woodcock, partridge or pheasant: lay the bird on its back. Remove skin from breast and with a very sharp knife cut out the white meat, including the top section of the wing, with the bone, as far down as the first joint. Lift out small fillet carefully. Remove any sinews and pound the fillet to about ¼″ thickness. The bone is removed except when filleting chicken for à la Kiev.

If you have an obliging butcher you may be able to persuade him to do this for you.

CHICKEN À LA KIEV
(*Kievskiye Kotletki*)
FOR 4 SERVINGS

¼ *lb butter*, very *cold*
4 *fillets of chicken, with bone*
½ *teaspoon salt*
2 *eggs*
¼ *cup milk*
1½ *cups breadcrumbs*
2–3 *cups chicken fat or oil for deep frying*

Cut the butter into strips about 3″ long and ½″ thick. Put it in the refrigerator. It must be kept absolutely cold and hard until the moment of using.

Sprinkle the Kiev fillets with salt, lay them on the table, pound lightly, and in the centre of each put a strip of cold butter (1). Roll the flesh round the butter (2), leaving the wing-bone projecting like the stalk of a pear. Be sure the butter is completely sealed inside the fillet. Dip into egg beaten with milk, roll in breadcrumbs, dip in egg again and roll again in crumbs. Deep fry in hot fat for 4 or 5 minutes. The fillets must be served immediately they are ready. French-fried or mashed potatoes, green peas, carrots or cauliflower dusted with fried breadcrumbs are good accompaniments for this dish.

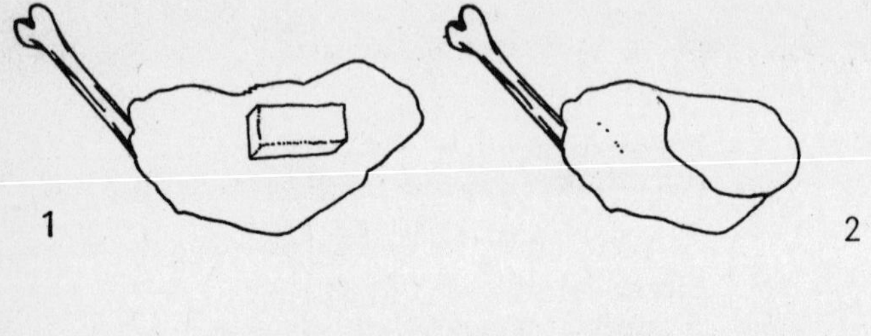

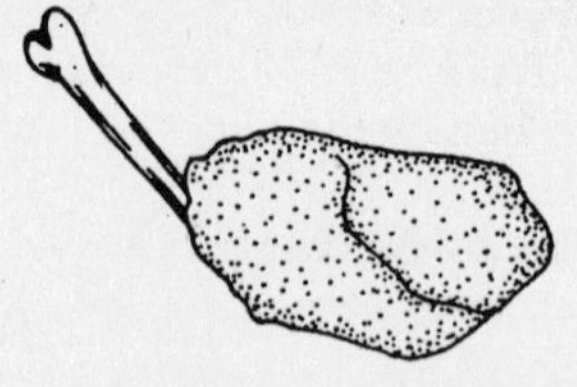

CHICKEN FILLETS IN BREADCRUMBS

(*Fille Zeplyonka v Suharyakh*)

FOR 4 SERVINGS

This is a very much simpler preparation than Kiev Chicken.

4 *chicken fillets cut from the chicken without the wing-bone (see preparation of Poultry and Game for Chicken à la Kiev* (*)
1 *teaspoon salt*
1 *egg*
1 *cup breadcrumbs*
¼ *pound butter* or ½ *cup oil for frying*

Sprinkle the fillets with salt, dip them into the beaten egg and roll in breadcrumbs. Melt the butter or oil in pre-heated pan and fry for 5–7 minutes. Serve immediately with french-fried potatoes, green peas, young buttered carrots or cauliflower dusted with fried breadcrumbs.

CHICKEN AND MUSHROOMS IN SOUR-CREAM SAUCE

(*Zeplyonok s Gribami v Smetane*)

FOR 4 SERVINGS

1 chicken weighing about 2½ pounds
1½ teaspoons salt
enough water to cover chicken
1 pound mushrooms
1½ tablespoons butter
1 cup sour cream

Put the chicken with the salt into cold water, bring to the boil, turn down heat and simmer until tender, about 40 minutes. When cool, cut it into pieces, removing all bones and skin. Coarsely slice the mushrooms and lightly fry in butter. Add the sour cream. Add the chicken and mix together. Remove from the heat and let it stand on the stove in a warm place for 5 minutes, keeping hot but not cooking. Serve with boiled rice or mashed potatoes.

BOILED FOWL FRIED IN BREADCRUMBS

(*Kuritza v Suharyakh*)

FOR 6 SERVINGS

1 boiling fowl, about 3 pounds
enough water to cover fowl
1 tablespoon salt
3 peeled carrots
1 onion
2 eggs
½ cup milk
2 cups breadcrumbs
4 tablespoons butter for frying

Put the fowl in cold water with the salt, carrots and onion, bring to the boil, reduce heat and simmer for 2–2½ hours. Leave it to cool in its stock, which makes it juicier. When cold, take it out, cut it in pieces, dip it in beaten egg and milk and roll in breadcrumbs. Fry quickly in butter. Serve with french-fried potatoes and the re-warmed carrots which were cooked with the fowl.

This may be served as a zakuska and eaten hot or cold.

FOWL WITH RICE AND WHITE SAUCE

(*Kuritza s Risom i Belim Sousom*)

FOR 6 SERVINGS

1 *boiling fowl of 3–4 pounds*
enough water to cover fowl
1 *tablespoon salt*
3 *carrots*
1 *onion*
6 *cups hot boiled rice* (*)

For sauce

2 *tablespoons plain flour*
½ *cup water*
2 *tablespoons sour cream*
juice of ½ lemon

Put the fowl in cold water with the salt, carrots and onion, bring to boil, then simmer for 2–2½ hours. Keep hot in the stock. Take 2 cups of this chicken stock and put into a separate saucepan and bring to the boil. Mix together the flour and ½ cup of water, pour it into the stock, stirring all the time, and add the sour cream. Bring just up to the boil Add lemon juice. Arrange the hot boiled rice on a dish and set the pieces of fowl round it. The sauce is served separately or poured over all.

CHAHOHBILI OF CHICKEN

(*Chahohbili*)

FOR 4 SERVINGS

1 *chicken, weighing about* 2–2½ *pounds*
2 *tablespoons butter*
1 *large onion, chopped*
1 *teaspoon salt*
pepper
1 *bay leaf*
½ *cup tomato sauce*
1 *cup chicken stock*
juice of ½ lemon
2–3 *medium-sized tomatoes*
1 *tablespoon butter for frying tomatoes*

This Caucasian dish comes from Georgia but is very popular in all parts of Russia.

Joint the chicken and fry it in 2 tablespoons butter. Add the onion and fry together till golden-brown. Put into a casserole with salt, pepper, bay leaf, tomato sauce and stock. Simmer for 20–30 minutes. Add the lemon-juice. Skin the tomatoes, cut in halves and fry in 1 tablespoon butter. Put the Chahohbili into a deep dish, arrange the tomatoes on top and serve with boiled rice.(*)

POULTRY RAGU

(Ragu iz Kuritzi)

FOR 6 SERVINGS

1 *chicken, about 2½–3 pounds weight*
2 *tablespoons butter for frying*
2 *cooking apples*
2 *peeled carrots*
1 *onion*
½ *pound mushrooms*
1 *peeled parsnip*
2 *potatoes*
½ *pound green peas*
½ *cup sultanas*
1½ *teaspoons salt*
1 *cup bouillon*

Cut the chicken into pieces and lightly fry in butter. Take from frying-pan and put into a casserole. Peel, wash and cut apples and all vegetables, except peas, into small dice. Fry lightly in the melted butter you used for the chicken. Put fried apples and vegetables into the casserole with the chicken, peas, sultanas, salt and bouillon. Cover and simmer for 30 minutes, till all is cooked. Serve with fried or boiled potatoes or boiled rice.

The same recipe may be used for boiling fowl, goose, duck, giblets or a combination of all these. If using boiling fowl it should be cooked for 1 hour before frying.

POULTRY KOTLETKI

(Kuriniye Kotletki)

FOR 3 SERVINGS

1½ *pounds chicken or fowl fillets*
1 *cup torn white bread soaked in milk and squeezed out*
1 *tablespoon butter*
1 *teaspoon salt*
1 *egg*
½ *cup breadcrumbs*
3 *tablespoons butter for frying*

Skin and remove all sinews from the fillets. Put fillets through the mincer 3 times. Add the squeezed-out bread, 1 tablespoon butter and salt. Mix all together thoroughly, form into oblong kotlets about 3½″ long and ½″ thick. Dip in beaten egg, roll in breadcrumbs and fry in butter. Serve with boiled carrots, green peas and fried potatoes.

ROAST TURKEY WITH CHESTNUTS AND APPLES

(*Indyushka s Kashtanami i Yablokami*)

FOR 8–10 SERVINGS

1 turkey, weighing about 8 pounds
1 tablespoon salt

For filling
1½ cups apple purée
3 cups unsweetened chestnut purée
2 tablespoons butter or fat for roasting

For gravy
½ cup bouillon
1 tablespoon flour

Preheat oven to Reg. 6: 400°. Prepare the turkey for roasting and rub it with salt inside and out. Mash together the apple and chestnut purée and stuff the turkey. Sew up the opening and roast in butter or poultry fat, basting occasionally. The roasting time will vary with the size of the turkey but an 8-pound bird takes about 2–2½ hours in a hottish oven. A larger bird will take longer. Test for readiness by piercing the thickest part of the leg. If the juice that comes out is not red and the meat is tender the bird is ready.

Keep the turkey hot on a large dish and make the gravy by adding the bouillon and flour to the liquid in the roasting-pan, after straining off excess fat. Serve with boiled buckwheat (*), french-fried potatoes, green peas and boiled carrots.

If tinned chestnut purée is not available or if fresh chestnuts are preferred, make the stuffing the following way:

FRESH CHESTNUT STUFFING

FOR 8–10 SERVINGS

enough chestnuts to fill the bird when mixed with apples
boiling water for blanching
1 cup milk
4 medium-sized apples
½ cup water
2 tablespoons butter
1 pinch of salt

Blanch the chestnuts with boiling water and take off the skins. Put them in a saucepan with the milk. Boil, covered, for 20–30 minutes. Peel, cut up and cook the apples on low heat, with ½ cup water, till soft. Put the chestnuts and apples through mincer, or mash them together, adding the butter and salt. Stuff the turkey, sew up and roast.

ROAST TURKEY WITH LIVER FILLING

(*Indyushka s Pechonkoi*)

FOR 8 SERVINGS

1 *turkey, about* 8 *pounds weight*
1 *tablespoon salt*

For filling

2 *eggs*
1 *pound calf liver*
3 *tablespoons butter*
1 *cup torn white bread, soaked in milk and squeezed out*
1 *teaspoon salt*
pepper
2 *tablespoons butter or poultry fat for roasting*

For gravy

1 *tablespoon flour*
½ *cup bouillon*

Preheat oven to Reg. 6: 400°. Prepare the turkey for roasting and rub with salt inside and out. Separate the egg yolks and whites. Cut the liver into pieces, removing all sinews. Fry lightly in 1 tablespoon butter, then put through the mincer twice with 2 tablespoons butter and the squeezed out bread. Add salt, pepper and the egg-yolks. Mix well. Beat the egg-whites stiffly and blend in carefully with the liver mixture.

Put this stuffing into the bird and sew up the opening. Do not pack the stuffing in too tightly, it swells in cooking. Put the turkey into a hottish oven with 2 tablespoons butter or poultry fat and baste about every 15–20 minutes. Cook approximately 2–2½ hours. When cooked keep the turkey hot on a dish while making the gravy. Add the flour and bouillon to the pan-juice, and boil it up to thicken.

ROAST DUCK WITH APPLES

(*Utka s Yablokami*)

FOR 6 SERVINGS

1 *duck,* 5 *pounds weight*
1 *tablespoon salt*
6 *small cooking apples*
2 *tablespoons butter or poultry fat for cooking*
1 *pound potatoes*
1 *pound sweet potatoes*
1 *cup bouillon or water*
1 *tablespoon sour cream*

Preheat the oven to Reg 6: 400°. Prepare the duck for roasting. Rub it with salt inside and out. Wash the apples and cut them in halves. Fill the duck with apples and sew it up. Put in the roasting-pan with butter or fat and roast in a hottish oven for 30 minutes. Add the potatoes and sweet potatoes and roast all together, basting occasionally, for another 1–½ hours.

When cooked, put the duck on a dish with apples on one side and potatoes on the other. Keep hot while you make the gravy by adding the bouillon and sour cream to the pan juice. Serve gravy in a sauce-boat.

This recipe could also be used with goose.

DUCK WITH STEWED CABBAGE

(*Utka s Kapustoi*)

FOR 4 SERVINGS

1 *duck, about 4 pounds weight*
1 *teaspoon salt*
2 *tablespoons butter for frying*
2 *cups bouillon or water*
1 *small cabbage*
1 *small onion*
2 *apples*
½ *teaspoon salt*

Cut the duck into large pieces, salt it and fry in butter till golden-brown. Put in a deep casserole with a lid, add a little of the bouillon or water, cover and simmer for 30 minutes.

Cut up the cabbage and onion and fry lightly in butter. Peel and slice the apples and add, with ½ teaspoon salt and the rest of the bouillon. Simmer till the cabbage is tender, about 30 minutes. Mix in with the duck and cook on low heat for another 30 minutes. Serve with boiled potatoes or boiled rice.

GOOSE WITH NOODLES

(*Gus s Lapshoi*)

FOR 8 SERVINGS

1½–2 *pounds of goose, cut in pieces*
3 *tablespoons butter*
1 *teaspoon salt*
1 *cup bouillon or water*
Garniture
dill or *parsley*
1 *pound egg noodles*
1 *teaspoon salt for noodles*
6 *cups water to boil noodles*

Brown the pieces of goose in butter, then add salt and bouillon and simmer in covered saucepan until the meat is cooked, approximately 1 hour. Put the noodles in boiling salted water, boil for 10 minutes, drain off, put them on top of the goose meat and simmer for 5–10 minutes. Arrange all in a deep dish, sprinkle with dill or parsley and serve as a complete course.

Game (Dich)

Russia has a wonderful variety of game which can be used for the table . . . wild duck, partridge, grouse, woodcock, hazel-hen, capercaillzie, hare, deer and even bear. Nina, who has eaten both, says that cured and smoked haunch of wild bear from Southern Russia is excellent but Siberian bears are tough.

In the old days bears were trapped by putting a copper jar with a narrow neck, baited with honey, near a den. The bear pushed his muzzle in to lick the honey and could not get his head out again.

PHEASANT
(*Faizan*)

FOR 4 SERVINGS

1 *pheasant*
3 *tablespoons butter*
1 *pound button mushrooms*
½ *pound small onions*
1 *teaspoon salt*
1 *cup bouillon*

Fry the pheasant in butter till golden-brown all over, then move into a deep casserole. Lightly fry the mushrooms and onions in butter used for pheasant, and spread them over the bird. Add salt and bouillon and simmer until cooked, about 45 minutes.

PHEASANT WITH MUSHROOMS IN SOUR-CREAM SAUCE
(*Faizan s Gribami v Smetane*)

FOR 4 SERVINGS

1 *pheasant*
2 *tablespoons butter*
1 *pound button mushrooms*
½ *cup bouillon*
1 *teaspoon salt*
1 *cup sour cream*

Cut the pheasant into pieces and fry them lightly in butter. Add the mushrooms, bouillon and salt. Simmer for 30 minutes. Add the sour cream, bring to the boil and simmer for 15 minutes. Serve with boiled rice or french-fried potatoes.

GAME BIRDS COOKED IN CLAY

This method is suitable for quail, plover, snipe, and is used by huntsmen.

Draw the birds, fill them with butter and salt, cover in clay and put in the fire. When the clay cracks the birds are ready. The feathers come off with the clay.

PREPARATION OF HARE, DEER, WILD PIG, BEAR, GOAT

To remove the strong flavour from the meat of wild animals, cut the meat into pieces weighing about 2–3 pounds and soak it in cold water for 3–4 hours. Then put it into cold Marinade for Game for 3 or 4 days, keeping it in the refrigerator.

MARINADE FOR GAME
(*Marinad dlya Dichi*)

3 *pints water*
1¼ *ounces acetic acid*, (33⅓% *strength*)
1 *tablespoon salt*
1 *tablespoon sugar*
2–3 *bay leaves*
1 *teaspoon peppercorns*
1 *onion*
1 *sprig parsley*

Acetic acid should be available from the chemist, but if unobtainable, white wine vinegar is an acceptable subtitute. Boil all the ingredients together for 10 minutes. Cool. Pour the mixture over the meat and put it in the refrigerator. Turn the meat occasionally. Leave at least 24 hours.

When it is needed for use take it out of the marinade, dry off with a cloth and cut it into pieces, whatever size you want.

Hare needs only 24 hours in the marinade and need not be cut up. The whole animal may be cooked. With other animals, usually the loin and hindleg only are used.

The flavour of deer, goat, hare or bear is improved if the meat is larded before cooking with strips of fresh pork fat, about ½ pound to every 4 pounds of meat.

FRIED HARE WITH SOUR CREAM

(*Zayetz Zharini v Smetane*)

FOR 4–5 SERVINGS

1 hare
¼ pound fat bacon, in strips
1 teaspoon salt
3 tablespoons lard or butter for frying
1 cup hot water
1 cup sour cream

Preheat the oven to Reg. 6: 400°. Lard the hare with fat bacon strips. Cut it into pieces, salt it and fry in hot fat until it is light brown. Put it into a casserole; swill round the frying-pan with the hot water and pour over the meat. Add the sour cream and cook slowly, covered, on top of the stove or in a medium oven, until the meat is tender, approximately between 45–60 minutes. Serve with french-fried potatoes, green beans or beetroots.

HARE FRIED IN BREADCRUMBS

(*Zayetz Zharini v Suharyakh*)

FOR 5–6 SERVINGS

1 hare
1 teaspoon salt
1 cup lard or butter
1 carrot
1 onion
1 cup bouillon
pepper
1 tablespoon flour
1–2 eggs
1 cup breadcrumbs

Preheat oven to Reg. 6: 400°. Prepare the hare, salt it and put it in a baking-dish with the fat. Brown it all over. Chop up the carrot and onion and add them, with the bouillon, to the hare. Add salt and pepper. Cover the dish and bake until the meat is tender, approximately 1½ hours. The time will vary with the size of the hare.

When cooked, take it out of the pan — leaving the carrot and onion in the pan — and let it cool. Meanwhile make a gravy by thickening the pan liquid (with carrot and onion) with flour, adding a little more bouillon or water if necessary. Stir well, bring to the boil, then keep warm.

Cut the hare into serving sections and just before serving dip them into beaten egg, roll in breadcrumbs, and fry in hot fat for a few minutes. Serve with french-fried potatoes, fresh green salad and tomatoes, with the gravy served separately.

TO ROAST WILD GOAT, PIG OR BEAR

Marinade the meat, as in Marinade for Game(*), lard it with fat bacon, then roast it in the oven at Reg. 8: 450°. Serve with any vegetables you like.

FILLET OF WILD DEER OR GOAT
(*Fille Dikoi Kozi ili Olenya*)

Marinade meat as in Marinade for Game (*). Lard the meat. Remove the bones from the loin and cut the meat into pieces about 1″ thick. Pound it lightly, salt it and fry.

Pies and Little Pies
(Pirogi i Piroshki)

Russians apply diminutive names not only to people and animals but also to inanimate objects, even pies. The word piroshki (baby pies) is the diminutive of pirog or pie.

Pirogi and piroshki are widely used in Russia for parties, picnics, lunches, snacks etc., for a meal on their own or served with soup. There is a great variety of fillings, the most popular being meat, cabbage, fish with vesiga, rice with mushrooms, shallots with egg, or mashed potato with bacon. Probably the most famous pirog outside Russia is Kulibyaka, made with salmon and eaten hot, and found on the menus of most good international restaurants.

Pirogi and piroshki are made with short pastry, with pancake and with yeast dough. They may be served hot or cold. There are also sweet pirogs of fruit or berries.

When making any sort of pies or little pies the fillings should be prepared before the pastry is made, not only so that the dough is not kept waiting but to ensure the filling is cold before being put in.

PIE WITH FISH FILLING
(Pirog s Riboi)

FOR 8–10 SERVINGS

For filling

1 4-*ounce packet dry Vesiga or transparent Chinese vermicelli*
(Vesiga is the dried marrow from the spine of the sturgeon. Substitute Chinese transparent vermicelli, made from green bean starch)

salted water for boiling vermicelli
1 *white onion*
4 *tablespoons butter*
1 *pound boned fresh fish such as cod, haddock or jewfish*
pepper
salt

For Short Pastry

¾ cup softened butter
1 *cup sour cream*
2 *whole eggs*
1 *egg yolk*
1 *teaspoon salt*
3 *cups plain flour*
2 *cups self-raising flour*
½ *cup fine breadcrumbs*
extra plain flour for pastry board
1 *egg for brushing pastry*

Preheat oven to Reg: 6: 400°. Make the filling first. Boil the vermicelli in *plenty* of salted water — it swells in cooking — for 20 minutes. Drain it well, put it in a bowl and chop with a knife. Chop the onion finely, fry it in butter and add to the vermicelli. Cut the fish in small pieces and mix in with onion and vermicelli, adding pepper and salt.

Tinned fish such as tuna or salmon could be used instead, with the liquid drained off, and boiled rice instead of vermicelli.

Now make the pastry. Put the butter, sour cream, egg and egg yolk into a bowl, add the salt and mix well together. Fold in first the plain flour, then the self-raising. Mix. Tip the dough out on a well-floured board, knead until smooth and even.

Take an oven-proof dish approximately 10″ × 12″, with sides 1½″ to 2″ high, butter it lavishly and sprinkle with fine breadcrumbs. Take two-thirds of the dough, roll it out to the size of the dish so the dough will line the sides. Flour the dough lightly, roll it over the rolling-pin, then unroll into the dish, trying not to tear it. Put in the cold filling, spreading it out evenly. Fold in the edges of the dough.

Roll out the rest of the dough and cover the top of the pie, joining all the edges together. Brush with beaten egg and sprinkle with breadcrumbs. Make a ½″ slit in the centre to let out steam and prevent the joins opening. Bake for 30–35 minutes at Reg. 6: 400°, until golden-brown all over. Take from the oven, cover with grease-proof paper and a cloth and let pie rest for 5 minutes; then slide it on to a board, cut in two lengthways and across 5 times. This makes pieces of approximately 2″ × 3″. Arrange on a dish and serve.

LITTLE PIES WITH SHALLOTS AND EGG FILLING

(*Piroshki s Lukom i Yaitzami*)

FOR 40–45 PIROSHKI

For filling
1 *bunch shallots*
2 *tablespoons butter*
8 *hard-boiled eggs*
1 *teaspoon salt*
pepper

For Short Pastry
Dough as for Pie with Fish Filling (*).

Preheat oven to Reg. 3–4: 350°. Make the filling first. Wash the shallots, shake off all the water and cut across into ½″ pieces. Melt the butter in frying-pan and fry shallots for 3 minutes. Chop up hard-boiled eggs very fine. Add shallots, with the butter they were fried in, plus salt and pepper, mixing all well together. Let it get cold.

Roll out the dough to less than ¼″ thickness. Cut it out in circles, using a glass or circular cutter about 3″–3½″ in diameter. Put a full teaspoon of filling in the centre of each circle and join the edges together down the middle, forming an oval. Flatten lightly and put on a buttered baking-sheet with the join underneath to prevent opening during cooking. Bake until golden-brown, approximately 15–20 minutes.

YEAST DOUGH PIE WITH MEAT

(*Pirog s Myasom*)

FOR 10–12 SERVINGS

For Meat Filling
1 *cup water*
1 *tablespoon salt*
pepper
2½ *pounds finely-minced beef*
½ *cup chopped onions*
1 *tablespoon butter for frying onions*
2 *tablespoons flour*

For Yeast Dough
1 *ounce fresh yeast*
½ *cup lukewarm water*
1½ *cups milk*
2 *eggs*
½ *cup butter*
2 *tablespoons oil*
1 *tablespoon sugar*
1 *teaspoon salt*
1¼ *pounds plain flour*

Preheat oven to Reg. 3–4: 350°. Make the filling first. Add water, salt and pepper to meat and mix well. Fry onions in butter till light brown. Add meat to onions, mixing all the time to avoid uncooked lumps. Fry about 10 minutes. When meat is almost cooked sprinkle half the flour on it and mix in well; then add the rest of the flour and mix again. Cook for 3 minutes. Remove from stove and leave to cool.

To make the dough, dissolve the yeast in ½ cup warm water. Mix together in a large bowl all ingredients except flour and yeast; then add yeast, then flour. Beat with a wooden spoon for 5–10 minutes, until the dough is thoroughly mixed and starting to form bubbles. It is essential to do this properly or it will be heavy. Cover the bowl with a clean cloth and allow the dough to rise until it has doubled itself in size. Tip it out on a floured board, knead it very lightly, then cut off one-third, reserving this for the top. Roll out the rest of the dough to the shape of a shallow pie-dish, about 8″ × 10″. Allow enough to cover the sides. Lay the dough in the pan, put in the filling, spreading it right to the edges. Turn the edges in over the filling; then roll out the rest of the dough, cover the top of the pie and join the edges together. Make a ½″ slit in the centre, for steam, brush with beaten egg and bake in a moderate oven, until the dough is cooked through, about 30 minutes. Test with a cake tester on the edge or corner of the pie crust and if pie is done take it from the oven, brush it with melted butter, cover with grease-proof paper and a light clean cloth. Leave for 5 minutes, then slide it onto a board, cut into oblong pieces and serve hot or cold.

DEEP-FRIED LITTLE PIES WITH CABBAGE

(*Zhariniye Piroshki s Kapustoi*)

FOR 25–30 PIROSHKI

For Cabbage Filling

1 *medium-sized cabbage*	2 *hard-boiled eggs*
enough water to cover cabbage	*salt*
1 *white onion*	*pepper*
½ *cup butter*	1 *teaspoon sugar*

(For these piroshki the cabbage filling should be made while the dough is rising.)

For Yeast Dough

1 *ounce fresh yeast*	1 *tablespoon sugar*
½ *cup lukewarm water*	½ *cup oil*
1¼ *cups milk*	1 *pound plain flour*
1 *egg*	3 *cups oil for deep-frying*
1 *teaspoon salt*	

To make filling, chop cabbage fine, put in saucepan, cover with water and bring to the boil. Cook for 5 minutes. Drain it off in a colander, carefully pressing out any remaining water; otherwise it will be too wet for frying.

Chop the onion and fry in butter till light brown. Add the cabbage and fry together for 10–15 minutes. Chill. Chop the hard-boiled eggs and add to cabbage with salt, pepper and sugar.

To make the dough, dissolve the yeast in ½ cup lukewarm water. Mix together all other ingredients except flour, then add yeast, then flour. Beat with a wooden spoon for 5–10 minutes, until the dough is thoroughly mixed and starting to form bubbles. Do not cut down on the beating time if you want the dough to be light. Cover the bowl with a clean cloth and leave dough to rise. When it has doubled its size, tip out on a well-floured board. Lightly sprinkle flour on top, cut out with a glass into small circles. The dough is very springy and if the glass is pressed straight down on it it will rise up inside. Cut down into the dough using first one side of the glass, then tilting it to cut with the other so the air can get out.

Flatten slightly on the board or by patting in your hands, into circles 3″–3½″ diameter, then put 1 tablespoon of filling in each. Fold over the dough and join the edges together, forming an egg-shaped pie with the join along the top. Put the piroshki on a floured board and let them rise for about 10 minutes.

In a saucepan heat 3 cups of oil to 400°, for deep-frying. When well-heated, drop in a small piece of dough. If it rises to the surface immediately the oil is hot enough. Deep-fry the piroshki, 4 or 5 at a time, turning them gently with a fork or pastry tongs, taking care not to pierce them. Cook until golden-brown, approximately 5 minutes, take them out, put them on paper to drain and cover with a cloth. Serve hot.

SUGGESTED VARIATIONS OF FILLINGS

RICE, EGG AND MUSHROOMS
(*Ris s Yaitzami i Gribami*)

1 pound fresh mushrooms
1 onion
½ cup butter
2 cups boiled rice
3 hard-boiled eggs, chopped
1 teaspoon salt
pepper

Clean, wash and chop the mushrooms. Chop onion and fry in butter. Add the mushrooms and fry until cooked almost dry. Mix with the rice and chopped eggs. Add salt and pepper to taste.

CARROTS WITH EGG
(*Morkov s Yaitzami*)

1½ pounds peeled raw carrots
1 onion
½ cup butter
6 hard-boiled eggs, chopped
1 teaspoon salt
pepper

Shred the carrots. Chop the onion and fry in half the butter. Add the carrots and the rest of the butter and fry together for 5–7 minutes, stirring lightly. Remove from heat and cool. Add chopped hard-boiled eggs, salt and pepper, mixing well together.

FRIED PANCAKE PIES
(*Blinchatiye Piroshki*)
FOR 5 SERVINGS

For Meat Filling
½ cup water
1 teaspoon salt
pepper
1½ pounds finely-minced beef
1 large onion
2 tablespoons butter for frying
1½ tablespoons flour

For Pancakes
3 eggs
1 cup milk
1½ cups plain flour
1 teaspoon salt
¾ cup water
4 tablespoons butter for frying

Make the meat filling first. Add water, salt and pepper to meat and mix well. Chop and fry the onions in butter till light brown. Add meat to onions, mixing all the time to avoid uncooked lumps and fry for about 10 minutes. When almost cooked sprinkle half the flour on meat and mix in well; then add the rest of the flour and mix again. Cook for 3 minutes. Remove from stove and leave to cool.

To make the pancakes, lightly beat the eggs and milk together. Sift the flour and salt together, add to eggs and milk and mix till smooth. Add water and mix again. In a hot frying-pan put ½ teaspoon butter. Pour in about 4 tablespoons of pancake mixture and cook on one side, then on the other till light brown. Drain on grease-proof paper. Continue process till all pancakes (blinchiki) are made.

Put 1 tablespoon of meat filling on each pancake, not quite in centre. Fold over a flap to cover filling, then fold in each side and finally roll up remaining side, making a kind of envelope. Five minutes before serving heat 1 tablespoon of butter in the frying-pan, put in the pies and brown all over. Serve hot, with broth, or as a light lunch or supper. This quantity should make 12–14 pies.

PANCAKE PIE
(*Blinchati Pirog*)
FOR 6–8 SERVINGS

Blinchati Pirog, a pie with layers of different fillings, is not difficult to make though it has a number of ingredients. Before starting, study the recipe carefully, then prepare the 3 fillings and let them cool while you make the pancakes and finally the pastry covering.

Cook the pie in a cake-tin, about 8″ across and 2½″ high, with or without removable sides. The pirog will come out firm and well-shaped and easy to cut.

For Meat Filling

½ cup water
½ teaspoon salt
pepper
¾ pound finely-minced beef
1 medium-sized onion
2 tablespoons butter for frying
1 tablespoon flour

For Mushroom Filling

2 cups coarsely chopped mushrooms
½ cup chopped onion
1 tablespoon butter

For Kasha Filling

1 cup boiled buckwheat (Kasha) (*)

For pancake layers

2 *eggs*
¾ *cup milk*
¾ *cup flour*
½ *teaspoon salt*
½ *cup water*
2 *tablespoons butter for frying*

For pastry case

2 *tablespoons softened butter*
2 *tablespoons sour cream*
2 *egg yolks*
½ *teaspoon salt*
1½ *cups plain flour*
1 *cup self-raising flour*
butter for greasing pan
¼ *cup fine breadcrumbs*

For sauce

1 *cup mushrooms, sliced and fried in butter*
1 *cup sour cream*

Preheat oven to Reg. 3–4: 350°. *Make the meat filling first.* Add water, salt and pepper to meat and mix well. Chop and fry the onion in butter till light brown. Add meat to onion, mixing all the time to avoid uncooked lumps and fry for about 10 minutes. When almost cooked sprinkle half the flour on the meat and mix it in well; then add the rest of the flour and mix again. Cook for 3 minutes. Remove from stove and leave to cool.

Make the mushroom filling. Melt the butter in frying pan, add chopped onion and fry for 2 or 3 minutes, then add chopped mushroom and fry another 4–5 minutes. Leave to cool.

Make 6 pancakes while the fillings are cooling. Lightly beat the eggs and milk together. Sift flour and salt together, add to eggs and milk and mix in till smooth. Add water and mix again. In a hot frying-pan put ½ teaspoon butter. Pour in about 4 tablespoons of pancake mixture and cook on one side, then turn and cook on the other side till light brown. Drain on grease-proof paper. Continue process till you have made 6 pancakes. Be sure they are not too big to fit into the cake tin.

Make the short pastry. Put butter, sour cream, egg and salt into a bowl and mix well together. Fold in plain flour, then self-raising flour. Mix well. Put dough on to floured board, knead till smooth. Cut off enough dough to cover top of pie and roll out the rest to ⅛″ thickness, big enough to line the cake-tin, including the sides. The dough should be in one piece, without joins. Butter the tin well, sprinkle with fine breadcrumbs and line it with the pastry.

Divide the meat filling into 3 parts. In the cake tin, which is already lined with pastry, spread one third of the meat filling.

Cover with a pancake and put half the boiled buckwheat filling on top. Cover with another pancake, put on half the mushroom filling and cover with next pancake. Repeat, finishing with a top layer of meat.

Roll out the rest of the pastry and cover the top layer. Join the edges securely and bake about 30 minutes in a moderate oven. When cooked, remove the sides from the cake-tin and turn pie upside-down on a serving dish. If the tin has no removable sides, just reverse it on to the dish and gently ease the pie out. Serve hot. Cut from the centre down, with a sharp pointed knife, like cutting a cake, and pour over the sauce of fried mushrooms heated in the sour cream.

This is usually a complete course, but if it is to be eaten with soup the sauce will not be needed.

CHICKEN, RICE AND EGG PIE

(*Kurnik*)

FOR 8–10 SERVINGS

For filling

1 boiled chicken weighing about 2 pounds
2 tablespoons butter
3 cups boiled rice
5 hard-boiled eggs
1 teaspoon salt
pepper

For pastry

Short Pastry as for Pie with Fish Filling (*)

For sauce

2 cups chicken stock
2 tablespoons flour
½ cup water
2 tablespoons sour cream
juice of ½ lemon

Garniture

dill

Preheat oven to Reg. 3–4: 350°. Cut up the cooked chicken meat into pieces about 1″ square and lightly fry them in butter. Mix with the boiled rice and chopped egg, adding salt and pepper. Chill.

Roll out the pastry, reserving one third for the pie top. Line an 8″ × 10″ pie dish with pastry and put in the filling. Roll out the rest of the dough, cover the pie and pinch the edges together.

Bake in a moderate oven for 20–25 minutes. Serve hot with sauce and sprinkled with dill.

For the sauce, boil up the chicken stock. Mix together flour and water and pour into stock, stirring constantly. Add the sour cream. Bring just up to the boil, add lemon juice and serve.

HOT SALMON PIE

(*Kulibyaka*)

FOR 8–10 SERVINGS

Though this famous fish pie is made with the same short pastry as Kurnik and other pies it is higher and narrower in shape. It should be made with fresh salmon but tinned salmon or tuna may be substituted.

For filling

1 4-*ounce packet Vesiga or Chinese transparent vermicelli*
Salted water for boiling vermicelli
1½ *pounds salmon*
¼ *pound butter*
1 *large onion*
½ *pound mushrooms*
1 *tablespoon parsley, chopped*
3 *hard-boiled eggs, chopped*
1 *beaten egg*
¼ *cup breadcrumbs*

For pastry

Short Pastry as for Pie with Fish Filling (*)
2 *tablespoons hot melted butter*

Preheat oven to Reg. 6: 400°. Prepare the vermicelli. Put it into large saucepan of boiling water (it swells in cooking), reduce heat and cook for 20 minutes. Drain well, put in a bowl and chop up with a knife. Let it cool.

Cut the salmon into pieces, coat it in melted butter and allow to cool and stiffen.

Chop the onion and mushrooms. Fry onion in butter; add mushrooms and toss together. Cool. Add chopped parsley.

Roll out the dough into a large square, about ¼″ thick. Lay it in a buttered pie pan. Arrange the filling down the centre of the dough in layers . . . salmon, vesiga, mushrooms with onion, chopped egg and parsley. Fold over the dough, joining it down the centre of the pie and forming an oblong. Seal the ends. Make a half-inch slit to let out steam in cooking. Brush with beaten egg, sprinkle with breadcrumbs and bake in Reg. 6: 400° oven for

30–35 minutes, till golden-brown. If you want to be specially lavish, pour 2 tablespoons of hot melted butter into the slit in the pie crust when you take it from the oven. Cut across into 2″ pieces and serve hot.

As with most of Russia's best dishes, preparation of Kulibyaka is simple but only the finest possible materials are used.

Light Meals and Luncheon Dishes (Lyohkye Blyuda dlya Posdnego Zavtraka)

Though some of the recipes in this chapter may seem similar to those of other countries they taste unmistakably Russian because of such typical ingredients as dill or sour cream or the combination of sour cream and mushrooms. In the same way, though the origins of the stuffed vegetables may be traced back to the Caucasus and Middle East, the fillings have become essentially Russian.

In a Russian household such dishes would be eaten at lunchtime or perhaps some of the stuffed vegetables might be served cold, as zakuski. They make a pleasant light meal with a salad and cheese or fresh fruit.

STUFFED TOMATOES WITH VEAL AND RICE
(*Pomidori Farshirovaniye Telyatinoi s Risom*)

FOR 4 SERVINGS

8 *tomatoes*
boiling water

For filling

½ *cup chopped onion*
3 *tablespoons butter*
½ *pound minced veal, uncooked*
1 *cup boiled rice*
½ *teaspoon salt*
pepper
¼ *cup tomato sauce*

Garniture

dill or *parsley*

Choose tomatoes that are ripe but not soft, as even as possible in shape and size. To skin, dip them in boiling water for half a minute, take out with a slotted spoon and peel with a pointed knife. Cut off the top and with a small spoon remove the inside and put it aside. Try not to cut the tomato case.

Stuffed tomatoes should be cooked in the dish in which they are to be served, for they are very soft and may break or lose their shape if handled too much.

To make the Veal and Rice filling, fry half the onion in 1 tablespoon butter. Add meat and fry together. Take off heat and add boiled rice, salt and pepper. Mix well, add tomato sauce and fill the tomato cases. Put in a casserole. Fry the rest of the onion and add chopped tomato centres. Fry for 5 minutes, then add them to the tomatoes in their dish and simmer for 20 minutes, covered. Sprinkle with dill or parsley and serve hot.

ALTERNATIVE FILLINGS:

(*All quantities to fill* 8 *tomatoes*)

EGG AND MUSHROOM (*Yaitza s Gribami*)

½ *cup chopped onion*
3 *tablespoons butter*
½ *pound mushrooms*
6 *hard-boiled eggs, chopped fine*
½ *teaspoon salt*
pepper
½ *cup bouillon or water*
½ *cup fresh or sour cream*

Garniture
dill or *parsley*

Preheat oven to Reg. 3–4: 350°. Fry the onion in 2 tablespoons butter until light brown. Cut up the mushrooms, add to the onion and fry together. Remove from the heat and put aside half the mushrooms. To the remainder add finely-chopped hard-boiled egg, salt and pepper. Mix well and fill the tomato cases. Arrange them upright in an oven-proof dish, add bouillon and the rest of the butter and cook on low heat, covered, for 10 minutes.

Add fresh or sour cream to the rest of the mushrooms, bring them to the boil, pour mixture over the tomatoes and put in the oven for 10 minutes. Sprinkle with chopped dill or parsley and serve.

FRIED FISH IN SOUR CREAM FILLING
(*Riba v Smetane*)

1 *pound fish such as cod, haddock, or jewfish*
salt
½ *cup flour*
½ *cup oil*
1½ *cups sour cream*
½ *cup bouillon*
2 *tablespoons butter*

Remove the skin and bones from the fish and cut into pieces. (If using filleted fish it may be fried whole.) Salt it, roll in flour and fry in oil until cooked. Take off the stove and break up into smaller pieces. Mix in with the sour cream and fill the tomato cases. Arrange them standing upright in a saucepan, add the bouillon and butter and cook gently, covered, for about 15 minutes.

Tomato sauce could be used instead of sour cream.

PEPPERS STUFFED WITH MEAT
(*Peretz Farshirovani Myasom*)

FOR 4 SERVINGS

For filling

1 *pound finely-minced beef*
1½ *cups boiled rice*
½ *cup chopped onion fried in butter*
1 *cup water*
1 *teaspoon salt*
pepper

For pepper cases

8 *medium-sized green peppers*
2 *cups peeled and shredded carrots*
¼ *cup oil*
1 *cup tomato purée*
1 *cup water*

Make the filling first, by mixing together all the ingredients. Cut the tops off the peppers, removing all seeds, and fill with meat mixture. Stand upright in a saucepan.

Fry shredded carrots in oil for 5 minutes, then add the tomato purée and water. Mix well. Pour over the peppers and bring to the boil. Turn the heat down and simmer for 45 minutes.

VEGETABLE MARROW STUFFED WITH MEAT (*Kabachok Farshirovani Myasom*)

FOR 4 SERVINGS

2 *marrows, about* 8–10 *inches long*
butter for greasing pan
1 *teaspoon salt*
pepper
1 *pound finely-minced meat*
1 *sliced onion fried in butter*
1 *cup boiled rice*
2 *cups sour cream*

Garniture

dill or *parsley*

Preheat oven to Reg. 3–4: 350°. Peel the marrows and cut them into 4 parts, cross-ways, making slices about 2″ thick. With a spoon or knife, remove the centres. Set each piece upright, like a cup, on a well-buttered baking-dish. Salt and pepper them lightly.

Mix together the meat, fried onion, boiled rice and add seasoning to taste. Pile into the marrow slices and bake in a moderate oven for approximately 30–35 minutes. Pour the sour cream over and leave in the oven for a few more minutes. Sprinkle with dill or parsley.

VEGETABLE MARROW WITH VEGETABLE FILLING (*Kabachok Farshirovani Ovoschami*)

FOR 4 SERVINGS

2 vegetable marrows, cut and scooped out as for Vegetable Marrow Stuffed with Meat (*)

For filling

½ cup chopped onion
3 tablespoons butter or ½ cup oil
1 cup diced cooked carrots
½ cup diced cooked swede or turnip
1 cup diced cooked potatoes
1 teaspoon salt
pepper
1 tablespoon grated parmesan cheese
2 cups white sauce (*)

Preheat oven to Reg. 3–4: 350°. Fry the onions in oil or butter till golden-brown. Add the carrots and swede or turnip and fry together for a few minutes. Take off the stove and add the potatoes, salt and pepper. Mix well but do not mash up. Fill the marrows, sprinkle cheese on top and bake for about 15–20 minutes, until cooked through and brown on top. Serve with white sauce.

FRIED VEGETABLE MARROW (*Kabachok Zharini*)

FOR 2 SERVINGS

1 vegetable marrow, not too old
½ teaspoon salt
½ cup flour
2 tablespoons butter for frying

Peel the marrow and cut into rings about ½″ thick. Salt them, roll in flour and fry in hot butter till cooked. Serve as accompaniment to meat or as a separate dish. The marrow must be young. The same recipe may be used for aubergine, but they should be ripe, otherwise they will have a bitter taste.

SAUERKRAUT WITH MUSHROOMS
(*Kvashenaya Kapusta s Gribami*)

FOR 4 SERVINGS

1 cup dried mushrooms
2 cups water
1 pound sauerkraut
1 cup sour cream
1 teaspoon sugar

Wash the mushrooms, then soak them in 2 cups water for 1 hour; cook them for 15 minutes in the same water. Take them out and chop them fine. Add them to the sauerkraut with 1 cup of the water in which they cooked. Cook for 20 minutes. Add sour cream and simmer for another 20 minutes. Taste, and if too sour, add 1 teaspoon sugar. Serve hot with meat dishes.

Taste this recipe for salt as you proceed.

MUSHROOMS IN CREAM SAUCE
(*Gribi v Souse*)

FOR 2 SERVINGS

½ pound young mushrooms
1 tablespoon butter
¼ teaspoon salt
pepper
1 cup white sauce (*)
½ cup fresh cream
1 teaspoon lemon juice
dill or *parsley*

Clean, wash and slice the mushrooms. Put in a pan and fry lightly with butter. Add salt, pepper, white sauce and cream. Simmer, covered, for 5 minutes. Add the lemon juice, sprinkle with dill or parsley and serve as an accompaniment to meat, or on toast as a separate dish.

FRIED MUSHROOMS WITH ONION AND SOUR CREAM (*Gribi v Smetane*)

FOR 2 SERVINGS

½ cup chopped onion
2 tablespoons butter
½ pound mushrooms
¼ teaspoon salt
pepper
½ cup sour cream

Fry the onion in butter. Add sliced mushrooms and fry together for 5 minutes. Add salt and pepper and sour cream. Bring to the boil and serve as an accompaniment to meat or as a separate dish.

SCRAMBLED EGGS WITH FRANKFURTERS (*Yaichnaya Kashka s Sosiskami*)

FOR 2 SERVINGS

3 *frankfurter sausages*
1 *tablespoon butter*
4 *eggs*
½ *cup milk*
¼ *teaspoon salt*
pepper
dill
tomato sauce or 2 *fresh tomatoes*

Slice frankfurters in half-inch pieces. Fry lightly in butter. Beat egg and milk together and add salt and pepper. Pour over the frankfurters, stirring all the time until cooked. Sprinkle with dill and serve with tomato sauce or fresh slices of tomato.

You could use bacon, ham or salami as variations.

OMELETTE WITH SOUR CREAM SAUCE (*Omlet v Smetanom Souse*)

FOR 2 SERVINGS

The sauce must be made first so the omelette is not kept waiting.

For sauce

1 *tablespoon butter*
1 *tablespoon flour*
1 *cup hot milk*
1½ *cups sour cream*
2 *egg yolks*
¼ *teaspoon salt*
pepper

For omelette

4 *eggs*
½ *cup milk*
¼ *teaspoon salt*
pepper
¼ *cup chopped dill or parsley*
1 *tablespoon butter*

To make sauce, melt the butter in a saucepan and add the flour, stirring in carefully. Draw off the fire and add the hot milk, stirring to avoid lumps. Mix sour cream and egg yolks together and stir in carefully, adding salt and pepper. Simmer, stirring all the time, until the mixture becomes thick. Do not let it boil.

Beat together all omelette ingredients except the butter. Heat half the butter in frying-pan and pour in half the egg mixture. Cook quickly on one side, then turn omelette over and cook other side or put it under griller to brown. Put on a hot plate and immediately make the second omelette. Pour the sour cream sauce over each omelette and serve.

EGGS IN MASHED POTATO RINGS

(*Kartofelnoye Koltzo s Yaitzom*)

FOR 2 SERVINGS

1 tablespoon butter
1 tablespoon breadcrumbs
1½ cups mashed potato
4 eggs
¼ teaspoon salt
pepper
4 round slices of tomato
parsley

Preheat oven to Reg. 6: 400°. Butter a baking-dish and sprinkle it well with breadcrumbs. With a pastry-tube make 4 rings of mashed potato, about 3″–3½″ across in the centre. Brush them with melted butter, sprinkle with breadcrumbs and bake until light brown, approx. 10 minutes. Break one egg into the centre of each ring, add salt and pepper and bake until the eggs are cooked, about 7 minutes. Decorate with tomato slices and parsley. Serve hot.

EGG CROQUETTES

(*Kroketi iz Yaitz*)

FOR 2 SERVINGS

4 hard-boiled eggs
2 raw eggs
½ teaspoon salt
pepper
¼ cup thick white sauce
1 tablespoon milk
½ cup breadcrumbs
2 cups oil or lard for deep-frying
white bread for toast

Mash the hard-boiled eggs thoroughly and mix with one of the raw eggs. Season with salt and pepper and add to the thick white sauce. Roll into small balls the size of a walnut and dip them into the remaining egg which has been beaten with milk. Roll in breadcrumbs and deep-fry for 3 minutes, until golden-brown. Serve on small pieces of white toast or piled on a plate as zakuski.

Kasha (Buckwheat)

Kasha is very important in Russian cooking. Though usually taken to mean cooked buckwheat the word kasha is also used for other cooked grain — rice (risovaya kasha), semolina (mannaya kasha), oats (ovsyanaya kasha), millet (pshonaya kasha) etc. The nearest translation in English would be porridge. Since cooked buckwheat is so cheap, nourishing and full of vitamins it has been the mainstay of countless poor, old and sick Russians, and the word kasha has come to be used for it though its correct name is grechnevaya kasha.

Kasha is used in substantial dishes or as an accompaniment or stuffing for meat or poultry. It is also used as a breakfast food, prepared as a sweet or savoury dish, or boiled and eaten with butter. The Russians say, 'Kasha can't be spoilt by too much butter.'

BOILED BUCKWHEAT
(*Grechnevaya Kasha*)

1 *pint water*
salt
8 *ounces buckwheat*

Bring the water to the boil, add the salt and pour in the buckwheat, stirring with a spoon. Bring to the boil again, cover and simmer on very low heat for 40–50 minutes. When ready the kasha should be soft right through but not mushy. Each grain should be separate. This quantity makes about 1 pound cooked kasha.

Officially, that is how Nina cooks it, but some Russian women cook it this way: 'Boil the water, put in the kasha and boil till the water is evaporated. Put the lid on tight, roll the saucepan in thick newspapers, blankets, eiderdowns and between pillows and let it finish cooking itself. One babuska once surprised her foreign friends by getting up from the table and saying, 'I go now to get the kasha from my bed.'

BUCKWHEAT WITH BACON OR HAM
(Kasha s Vetchinoi)
FOR 4 SERVINGS

¾ pound bacon or ham
1 tablespoon butter
4 cups boiled buckwheat
1 chopped hard-boiled egg

Cut the bacon or ham into 1″ pieces and fry in butter. Put the boiled buckwheat on a hot dish and lightly mix in the bacon. Sprinkle with chopped egg and serve. As a variation the kasha could be eaten with fried onions and butter.

BUCKWHEAT WITH CREAM CHEESE
(Kasha s Tvorogom)
FOR 4 SERVINGS

2 cups buckwheat
½ pound cream cheese
1 teaspoon caraway seeds
1 cup fresh cream

Boil the buckwheat as for Boiled Buckwheat and as soon as ready mix in the cream cheese and caraway seeds. Try not to mash it up. Then pour the cream over it and put on very low heat for 10 minutes. Serve hot.

Rice (Ris)

The Russians use rice a great deal, for garnishing, for soups, for fillings and in sweet dishes. It features in certain traditional customs, for instance in Kutiya, served on Christmas Eve, at the end of the Advent Fast, and at Orthodox funerals, when sweetened rice is dealt out to the mourners.

BOILED RICE
(Risovaya Kasha)
FOR 4 SERVINGS

1 cup long rice
8 cups boiling water
1 tablespoon salt

Drop rice into boiling water, add salt and boil rapidly, uncovered, for 15–20 minutes. Drain water off in colander, then pour 2 cups boiling water over rice to remove the loose starch and separate the grains. Put rice back into saucepan and stand on low heat for 3 minutes to dry out moisture. The grains should be separate.

This makes 4 cups boiled rice.

PILAFF WITH EGG AND BACON OR HAM

(*Plov s Yaitzami i Vetchinoi*)

FOR 4 SERVINGS

2 *eggs*
¼ *cup milk*
1½ *tablespoons butter*
½ *pound bacon or ham*
3 *cups boiled rice*
salt to taste
pepper
dill

Preheat oven to Reg. 6: 400°. Mix eggs and milk together and make an omelette. Cut it into small pieces. Cut up the bacon or ham and fry lightly. Mix omelette and bacon with the rice, add salt and pepper, put it in the oven for about 10 minutes, in a covered dish. Sprinkle with dill before serving.

NOODLES WITH CREAM CHEESE

(*Lapsha s Tvorogom*)

FOR 4 SERVINGS

½ *pound broad noodles*
5 *cups boiling water*
1 *tablespoon salt*
½ *pound cream cheese*
2 *tablespoons butter*

Put noodles in boiling salted water and boil till tender. Drain off and while still hot mix in the cream cheese and butter. Serve hot.

NOODLES, SAILOR-STYLE

(*Lapsha po Flotski*)

FOR 4 SERVINGS

½ *pound noodles*
5 *cups boiling water*
1 *tablespoon salt*
½ *chopped onion*
2 *tablespoons butter*
½ *pound bacon or ham*
pepper

Put the noodles into the boiling salted water, boil till tender, then drain off and keep hot. Cut up the bacon or ham, fry the onion in butter and add the bacon or ham. Fry lightly together, then mix in with the noodles. Add pepper to taste and serve hot.

MACARONI BAKED WITH MEAT, EGG AND CHEESE (*Zapekanka s Myasom*)

FOR 4 SERVINGS

½ pound macaroni
6 cups boiling water
1 tablespoon salt
½ cup chopped onion
1½ tablespoons butter
½ pound minced meat
1 teaspoon salt
pepper
2 eggs
¼ cup milk
½ cup grated cheese

Preheat oven to Reg. 3–4: 350°. Put the macaroni into boiling salted water and boil till tender. Drain off and keep hot. Fry the onion in butter, add the meat and fry together till cooked, stirring to avoid lumps. Add salt and pepper. Mix in with the cooked macaroni, and put into a shallow buttered roasting-pan or oven-proof dish. Beat the eggs and milk together, pour over the meat, smooth out the top and sprinkle with cheese. Bake until the eggs are cooked, about 20 minutes. Eat hot with tomato sauce served separately.

Sweet Light Meals (Sladkiye Lyohkiye Blyuda)

It is not uncommon for a light meal to consist of a sweet dish, nor for these same dishes to be used as a sweet course in a dinner. Most of the following recipes could also be used as desserts.

SWEET RICE (*Risovaya Kasha, Sladkaya*)

FOR 4 SERVINGS

2 cups milk
½ cup long-grain rice
½ teaspoon salt
½ cup sugar
1 tablespoon butter
½ cup sultanas

Bring the milk to the boil. Add rice and salt, boil up again, turn down heat and simmer for 20 minutes, stirring occasionally. Add sugar, butter, sultanas. Mix and simmer for 5 minutes. Serve with extra hot milk if desired.

PILAFF WITH DRIED FRUIT
(*Plov Fruktovi*)
FOR 4 SERVINGS

½ cup dried apricots
½ cup stoned prunes
½ cup water
½ cup raisins
3 cups boiled rice
1½ tablespoons butter

Wash and cut up the apricots and prunes and cook together with the water, sugar and raisins for 10 minutes in a covered saucepan. Mix the rice with the cooked fruit and their juices, add the butter and serve.

BREAKFAST SEMOLINA
(*Mannaya Kasha*)
FOR 2 SERVINGS

2½ cups milk
½ teaspoon salt
½ cup semolina
½ cup sugar
1 tablespoon butter

Bring the milk to the boil and add the salt. Pour in the semolina, stirring fast so that no lumps can form. Simmer for 5 minutes, add the sugar and butter and serve hot. The longer you cook semolina the thicker it gets. Remedy this by adding more milk.

SEMOLINA PUDDING
(*Gurevskaya Kasha*)
FOR 6 SERVINGS

4 cups milk
½ teaspoon salt
½ cup semolina
1 tablespoon butter
½ cup sugar
½ cup blanched almonds, chopped
½ cup sultanas
½ cup glacé apricots, chopped
a few drops of vanilla essence
a few drops of almond essence
2 eggs
sugar for sprinkling on top of pudding

For Apricot Sauce
1 cup dried apricots
1½ cups cold water
¾ cup sugar

Preheat oven to Reg. 9: 500°. Bring the milk to the boil in a wide saucepan or casserole, then put it into the hot oven. Watch it carefully and when the top of the milk turns light brown push it down with a wooden spoon so that another top can form. When this is brown, push it down as before. Repeat this 5–6 times, for approxmately 20 minutes. Take milk from the oven, bring it to the boil on the top of the stove, add salt and semolina and cook on low heat, stirring all the time, for 10 minutes. Add the rest of the ingredients, except the eggs. Remove from heat. Separate egg yolks and whites. Beat the whites stiff, add the yolks and fold into the semolina mixture. Pour into 6 individual oven-proof dishes, sprinkle with sugar and put into a Reg. 6: 400° oven for 10 minutes. Serve hot, alone or with Apricot Sauce.

To make the sauce, wash the apricots in cold water, then put them in 1½ cups of cold water and leave for 2 hours. Cook them in the same water for 20 minutes. They should be soft. Put them through a fine sieve and then back into their cooking water. Add sugar, bring to the boil, stirring all the time since it burns easily.

MACARONI BAKED WITH FRUIT

(*Zapekanka s Fruktami*)

FOR 6 SERVINGS

½ *pound short macaroni*
4 *cups boiling water*
1½ *teaspoons salt*
1 *tablespoon butter*
1 *cup diced fresh apples*
½ *cup sultanas*
½ *cup mixed fruit peel*
2 *eggs*
½ *cup sugar*
1 *tablespoon butter for greasing pan*
1 *tablespoon breadcrumbs*
½ *cup jam*

Preheat oven to Reg. 3–4: 350°. Put macaroni into boiling salted water, boil till tender; then drain, add 1 tablespoon butter and let it cool. Add apples, sultanas and mixed fruit peel. Separate eggs and beat whites stiff. Add sugar and yolks and beat all together. Fold into macaroni and fruit, mixing gently. Put evenly into buttered and breadcrumbed baking-dish and bake in a moderate oven for 30 minutes. Serve hot with a teaspoon of jam on each helping.

YOGHURT PUDDING
(*Varenetz*)

FOR 4 SERVINGS

4 cups milk
½ cup sour cream
sugar for sprinkling

Preheat oven to Reg. 3–4: 350°. Heat the milk, put it in an oven-proof dish and set it in a moderate oven. When the top of the milk becomes golden-brown and starts to form a crust, push it down with a spoon and stir.

Repeat this process 4 or 5 times so that all the milk is eventually golden-brown, about 15–20 minutes. Take it from the oven and let it cool, stirring occasionally. Mix in the sour cream and leave it, at room temperature, until it becomes thick — about 4 to 5 hours. Put in the refrigerator. Serve cold with sugar sprinkled on top.

Using the same proportions, sour cream could be added to uncooked milk and left to set at room temperature. This makes a kind of yoghurt.

SWEET VARENIKI
(*Vareniki Sladkiye*)

FOR 10 SERVINGS

For berry filling
2 cups raspberries, cherries or blackberries
1 tablespoon sugar

For cream cheese filling
1 pound fresh unsalted cream cheese
1 egg
1 tablespoon sugar

For dough
3 eggs
2 cups milk
1 teaspoon salt
1½ pounds flour

For boiling Vareniki
4 cups boiling water

For sauce
1 cup sour cream

To make the berry filling, sprinkle the berries with sugar and leave to stand for 5 minutes. To make cream cheese filling just mix all the ingredients together.

To make the dough, beat eggs, milk, salt together in a mixing bowl; add flour, mix well together with a wooden spoon, turn out on a floured board and knead until springy. Make the vareniki in batches, cutting off a section of the dough and rolling it out about ⅛″ thick. Dust with flour, cut out in 2″ circles with a glass.

Put 1 teaspoon of filling in the centre of each circle, fold in half, pinch edges together. They should be half-moon shapes.

When ready the vareniki are dropped into boiling water and cooked till they rise to the surface. Serve 12–15 to each plate, with sour cream poured over.

CREAM CHEESE PATTIES
(*Sirniki*)

FOR 4 SERVINGS

¾ pound unsalted cream cheese
2 *eggs*
½ *cup flour*
½ *cup sugar*
1 *teaspoon vanilla essence*
flour for dusting
2 *tablespoons butter for frying*
1½ *cups sour cream for cooking*

Preheat oven to Reg. 3–4: 350°. Blend together all the ingredients except the sour cream for cooking and butter for frying. On a well-floured board, form mixture into round flat cakes about ½″ thick, 2″–2½″ in diameter. Be sure they are well-covered with flour. Melt butter in frying-pan and fry Sirniki on both sides until golden-brown. Arrange them flat on a buttered oven-proof dish which can be brought to the table, pour the sour cream over them and bake for 15 minutes in a moderate oven.

You could use fresh instead of sour cream and add ½ cup sultanas to give a sweeter flavour.

Sirniki, which look like small thick patties, must be made just before cooking, otherwise they become hard to handle. Once cooked they may be left for reheating just before serving.

SWEET CREAM CHEESE PASTE
(*Sladki Tvorog-pasta*)

FOR 2 SERVINGS

½ *pound unsalted cream cheese*
½ *cup sugar*
vanilla essence to taste

If the cheese is lumpy push it through a fine sieve with a wooden spoon, then mix in the sugar and vanilla. Pile it up into a pyramid on a glass plate and serve with stewed, dried or fresh fruit, berries or Kisel (*).

PANCAKE PIES WITH CREAM CHEESE

(*Blinchatiye Piroshki s Tvorogom*)

FOR 6 SERVINGS

For pancakes

3 *eggs*	½ *teaspoon salt*
1 *cup milk*	½ *cup water*
1½ *cups plain flour*	¼ *pound butter for frying*

For filling

1 *pound unsalted cream cheese*	1 *egg*
½ *cup sugar*	*vanilla extract*

For sauce

1½ *cups sour cream*	1 *tablespoon sugar*

Preheat oven to Reg. 8: 450°. To make the pancakes, lightly beat eggs and milk together. Sift together the flour and salt, add to egg and milk and mix in till smooth. Add the water and mix again. In a hot frying-pan put ½ teaspoon butter, pour in about 4 tablespoons of pancake mixture and cook on one side till light brown. Turn and cook on other side. Drain on grease-proof paper.

Make the filling by mixing together the cottage cheese, sugar and egg, adding vanilla to taste. Put 1 tablespoon of filling on each pancake, fold over a flap to cover filling, then fold in each side and roll up into a parcel, making a little pie or piroshki. Heat 1 tablespoon butter in the frying-pan, put in the pancakes and brown all over. When all are fried put them side by side in an oven-proof dish which can be brought to the table, mix together the sour cream and sugar, pour over the piroshki and bake in a hot oven for 10 minutes. Serve hot.

These piroshki can be served without oven-baking. The sour cream is poured over each one after frying and they are ready to eat.

APPLE CHARLOTTE WITH EGG SAUCE

(*Sharlotka i Gogol-mogol*)

FOR 8 SERVINGS

For Charlotte

butter for greasing dish
16 *slice of bread*, 4″ × 4″ × ¼″
3 *eggs*
½ *cup milk*
1 *tablespoon sugar*
3 *large cooking apples*
½ *cup raspberry jam*
½ *cup water*

For sauce

4 *egg yolks*
4 *tablespoons sugar*
1 *tablespoon rum*
vanilla essence to taste
2 *egg whites*

Preheat oven to Reg. 3–4: 350°. Butter an oven-proof serving-dish about 8″ × 8″. Toast the bread lightly. Beat the egg, milk and sugar together. Peel and slice apples, mix jam with the water. Dip 4 slices of bread into the egg mixture and arrange on the bottom of the dish. Evenly spread one third of the apples over them and pour one third of the jam mixture over all. Repeat this twice, covering finally with soaked bread. Bake for 30 minutes. Serve hot or cold.

To make the Gogol-mogol sauce, blend the egg yolks with the sugar until the sugar is almost dissolved. Add the rum and vanilla. Beat the egg-whites stiff and fold into the yolk mixture. Serve separately.

Puddings, Biscuits and Cakes
(Sladkoye Pecheniye i Torti)

Puddings and sweet dishes (Sladkiye Blyuda)

Puddings are not so popular in Russia as in England. After zakuski, soup and main course there is usually a pause, then coffee or tea, with torts, pastries or sweet little cakes, are served.

Russians have an almost oriental love of sweets. Sweet foods and honeyed drinks are mentioned even in the earliest records. This taste may have come from the East or from a natural bodily need for warmth and energy in a cold climate.

Some of the best desserts are made from fruit and berries, and variations of cream cheese mixtures. Most of these are adapted importations from Scandinavia or Germany, as for instance Kisel, a fruit-juice pudding which may have come with the Ruriks. It is almost identical with the Danish Röd Gröd and is also found in Poland and other Slav countries. Kisel may be made from all sorts of berries or fruits, or with flavoured milk or water. When using fruit and berries, potato-flour is better than cornflour because it does not change colour or affect the taste of the juice. It also makes the kisel clear.

Kisel is made either thin enough for pouring or thick enough for setting in a mould; but before making either kind the basic fruit juice must be prepared:

FRUIT JUICE FOR KISEL

For berries and fruit like black or redcurrants, cranberry, gooseberry, plums, sour cherries etc. allow ½ pound sugar to each 1 pound of fruit. For sweeter berries, use less sugar.

Wash the fruit or berries and remove any seeds. Crush with a wooden spoon. Add cold water, just covering the fruit, and simmer for about half an hour, until cooked. Strain thoroughly through a fine sieve, until the liquid is clear. Add the sugar and more water if necessary and bring to the boil. Thicken according to requirements.

KISEL FOR POURING

2 cups sweetened Fruit Juice for Kisel (*)
1½ tablespoons potato flour or cornflour
½ cup water

Bring the Fruit Juice for Kisel to the boil. Mix the potato flour or cornflour with the water and add, stirring all the time. When boiled, take off the stove and use as required.

RICE PUDDING WITH KISEL

(*Risovi Puding s Kiselem*)

FOR 6 SERVINGS

2½ cups milk
½ cup uncooked rice
pinch of salt
1 tablespoon butter
½ cup sugar
½ cup raisins
¼ cup orange peel
½ teaspoon vanilla essence
2 eggs — yolks and whites separated
Kisel for pouring (*)

Preheat oven to Reg. 3–4: 350°. To make the rice pudding, bring the milk to the boil. Add the rice and salt, bring to the boil again, reduce heat and simmer for 10 minutes. Remove from the stove, add the butter, sugar, raisins, orange peel, vanilla and egg yolks. Mix well. Beat the egg whites stiff and fold them in carefully. Put the mixture into an oven-proof buttered dish, smooth over the surface and bake for 15 minutes. Cut into sections or spoon out into individual dessert dishes. Pour the kisel over and serve.

SEMOLINA MOULD WITH KISEL

(*Manni Puding s Kiselem*)

FOR 6 SERVINGS

2½ cups water; or 1 cup of water and 1½ cups milk
½ teaspoon salt
½ cup semolina
½ cup sugar
1 tablespoon butter
Kisel for pouring (*)

Boil the water, or milk and water. Add the salt. Pour in the semolina, stirring fast to avoid lumps. Simmer for 8–10 minutes, then add sugar and butter. Cook a little longer, until it is really thick, then pour into a 2-cup mould, or small individual moulds, rinsed out with cold water. When set, unmould and pour kisel over before serving.

KISEL IN MOULD WITH WHIPPED CREAM

(*Kisel so Slivkami*)

FOR 6 SERVINGS

4 *cups sweetened Fruit Juice for Kisel* (*)
4 *tablespoons potato flour*
1 *cup water*
2 *cups fresh cream*
1 *teaspoon icing sugar*

Garniture
Fresh berries reserved from prepared fruit juice

Bring the Fruit Juice for Kisel to the boil, mix the potato-flour and water and add to juice, stirring all the time. Boil for 3 minutes. (This makes the kisel thicker.) Cool for 30 minutes. Rinse out a 5-cup ring-mould with cold water and pour in the mixture. Let it set.

Whip the cream with the sugar. Unmould the kisel, fill the centre with cream and decorate with fresh berries.

COFFEE PARFAIT

(*Parfe Koffeinoye*)

FOR 8 SERVINGS

2½ *cups fresh cream*
½ *cup freshly-ground coffee*
6 *egg-yolks*
1 *cup sugar*
1 *tablespoon gelatine*
½ *cup warm water*

Bring the cream to the boil. Add coffee, cover and put aside for just 30–45 minutes. Blend egg-yolks and sugar. Add strained coffee-cream. Dissolve the gelatine in warm water and pour it into the coffee mixture. Mix it in well. Rinse out a 5-cup mould with cold water, put in the coffee cream and stand in the refrigerator or freezer until it is set. It could be frozen like ice-cream or eaten just set firm. Unmould before serving.

FRUIT SURPRISE
(*Fruktovi Surpris*)
FOR 8 SERVINGS

1 tin mixed fruit cocktail — 30-ounce size
3 eggs
¾ cup sugar
1 tablespoon gelatine
¼ cup warm water
1½ cups fruit juice
2½ cups sour cream
½ teaspoon almond essence

Empty the liquid from the tin and strain it through a sieve. Separate the eggs and blend the yolks with the sugar. Dissolve the gelatine in the warm water. Put 1½ cups of the fruit juice, egg yolks and sugar, and gelatine into a saucepan and heat, stirring all the time. Do not boil. Remove from the heat and chill. Beat the whites of the eggs stiff, add the sour cream and almond extract. Beat again; then add to the chilled mixture. Mix together well. Add the strained fruit. Mix lightly. Rinse out a large mould with cold water, put in the mixture and allow to set.

ICE-CREAM
(*Plombir*)
FOR 8 SERVINGS

3 cups fresh cream
1½ tablespoons icing sugar
½ teaspoon almond essence
1 teaspoon vanilla essence
½ cup chopped glacé cherries
1 cup chopped glacé pineapple
½ cup chopped blanched almonds

Whip the cream and add the sugar, vanilla and almond essences. Fold in the glacé fruit and almonds, put the mixture into a mould or into individual dessert dishes and freeze until hard. Unmould by dipping the mould into warm water for a few seconds. Cut into sections with a warm knife and serve.

Biscuits and Cakes (Pecheniye i Torti)

BRANCHES

(*Hvorost*)

FOR 3 DOZEN BRANCHES

Hvorost are like Swedish Klenäter (Christmas Crullers) but are eaten without jam. They probably came from Scandinavia. The Russians always serve them at Christmas. They look rather like branches covered with snow and taste delicious.

4 egg yolks
⅓ cup fresh cream or tinned evaporated milk
¼ cup brandy
1½ teaspoons icing sugar
1½ cups plain flour
3 cups oil for deep frying
icing sugar for dusting

Mix together all ingredients except frying oil and dusting sugar. Stir until well blended. Turn the dough on to a floured board, knead, roll out very thin, rather less than ⅛″ thick. With a pastry-wheel cut strips about ¾″ wide and 3″ long. Cut a slit in the centre of each strip and twist one end through, making a kind of loose loop. Fry in deep oil, a few at a time, at about 375°, until light brown.

Put on a serving dish and dust with icing sugar while still hot. Pile them into a heap, dusting them as they come from the pan. Do not handle them too much, they break easily.

LITTLE STARS

(*Zvezdochki*)

FOR 3 DOZEN BISCUITS

4 egg yolks
1 cup sugar
1 teaspoon vanilla essence
1 cup unsalted butter
4 cups self-raising flour

Preheat oven to Reg. 3–4: 350°. Blend together the egg yolks and sugar. Add the vanilla essence. Melt the butter and add slowly. (It should not be *hot*.) Fold in the flour. The mixture should be quite firm. Put it into the refrigerator for an hour. Roll out to ¼″ thickness and cut the zvezdochki with a star-shaped cutter. Cook in a medium oven until golden-brown, approximately 10 minutes.

ALMOND FINGERS
(*Mindalniye Palchiki*)

FOR 2½ DOZEN BISCUITS

1¼ cups plain flour
3 tablespoons blanched and grated almonds
½ cup icing sugar
4 tablespoons unsalted butter
vanilla essence to taste
flour for dusting
butter for greasing pan
1 cup icing sugar for dusting biscuits

Preheat oven to Reg. ½–1: 250°. Mix together all ingredients except dusting flour, sugar, and butter for greasing. Mix with a knife on a pastry board, then knead as lightly as possible. Carefully, with the help of a knife, shape into little crescents about 1½″–2″ long. Do not use a biscuit cutter; the crescents should not be flattened. Put them on a buttered baking sheet, dust with flour and bake for about 30 minutes in a low oven. Watch them carefully to see they do not burn. Take them out and while still hot, dust and roll in icing sugar. Let them cool on a wire tray.

TRUMPETS WITH CREAM
(*Trubochki so Slivkami*)

FOR 12–14 TRUMPETS

4 egg whites
2 egg yolks
1 tablespoon unsalted butter, softened
½ cup sugar
¾ cup plain flour
butter for frying
2½ cups fresh cream for filling
icing sugar for dusting

Beat the egg whites stiffly. Cream the yolks, butter and sugar together. Add flour. Mix well, then fold in the egg whites. Heat frying pan, brush with melted butter and pour in about 2–3 tablespoons of the mixture, like a thin pancake. Fry lightly. Turn over and cook on the other side for a few minutes. Remove to a board, cut pancakes in halves and while still hot form each half into a trumpet or cone. Chill. Repeat process until all the mixture is used. Just before serving whip the fresh cream and fill the trumpets. Dust with icing sugar.

CREAM PUFFS

(*Pirozhnoe Zavarnoye s Zavarnim Kremom*)

FOR 30–35 PUFFS

1 *cup oil*
2 *cups boiling water*
2 *heaped cups plain flour*
1 *teaspoon sugar*
pinch of salt
6 *eggs* (*if small use* 8 *eggs*)
butter for greasing pan

Boiled Cream Filling

4 *cups milk*
4 *eggs*
2 *cups sugar*
1 *cup flour*
1 *teaspoon vanilla*
½ *cup unsalted butter*
1 *tablespoon icing sugar for dusting*

Preheat oven to Reg. 6: 400°. To make the cream puffs, boil the oil and water together. Remove from the heat and add flour, stirring in rapidly. Add sugar and salt. While still hot beat in eggs, one at a time, mixing well after each addition. Allow to cool for 2–3 hours, if possible in the refrigerator. On a greased baking sheet drop spoonfuls of mixture, about the size of half an egg or a large walnut. (Use a forcer if possible.) Bake in a 400–450° oven for 30–40 minutes. Do not open oven door for the first 20 minutes, while the puffs are rising, or they may collapse.

When cooked, cool them on a wire tray, then cut open at one side and add filling.

To make filling, boil 3 cups of the milk. Blend the eggs and sugar together and stir in the rest of the milk, flour and vanilla. Add this to the hot milk and pour into a double saucepan. Bring to the boil and keep boiling, stirring until thick. Cool till lukewarm. Beat in an electric mixer or by hand until creamy, adding butter. Be sure it is thoroughly blended. The butter should be softened before adding to facilitate mixing.

When the filling is cold, put it into the cold cream-puffs and dust with icing sugar.

NAPOLEON
(*Napoleon Tort*)

FOR ABOUT 24 NAPOLEONS

3½ cups plain flour
2 cups unsalted butter, at room temperature
1 cup sour cream
Boiled Cream Filling (*)
icing sugar for dusting

Preheat oven to Reg. 7: 425°. Put the flour on a board and cut the butter into it with a knife. Continue to cut till there are no large pieces of butter left. Add the sour cream and cut again, until all the flour is absorbed. Roll up the dough into a ball and put in the refrigerator overnight or for 12 hours. Then divide into 4 parts.

On a floured board, roll each part of dough separately, making 4 layers of about the same shape, about ⅛″ thick. Bake each layer separately on a flat buttered baking sheet about 14″ × 10″, for 10–12 minutes. The layers should be light golden in colour. Cool them and prepare the Boiled Cream Filling (*). Spread it evenly on each layer, putting one on top of the other, finishing with cream. Trim the edges with a sharp knife. Crumble up the cut-off edges and sprinkle on top of cream. Dust with icing sugar.

If you prefer, whipped fresh cream with a little sugar could be used instead of boiled cream.

FRUIT CAKE
(*Mazurka*)

FOR ABOUT 60 PIECES

This is another Christmas speciality, though it is also eaten at any time during the year. It is like Christmas cake made without spirits and with less flour. It is a flat shallow cake which does not rise at all. The eggs, flour and honey are mainly used to bind the fruit together. A good mazurka is rather moist.

2 cups mixed dried fruit — raisins, sultanas, currants, etc
1 cup dates
1 cup dried figs
½ cup glacé cherries
½ cup glacé pineapple
1 cup mixed glacé peel
1 cup blanched almonds, cut into threes
3 eggs
½ cup honey
1½ cups flour

Preheat oven to Reg. ½–1: 250°. Cut the dates, figs and glacé fruit into ½″ pieces. Mix all ingredients together thoroughly. Spread well-buttered grease-proof paper on a shallow baking-dish, about 10″ × 14″, then put in the mixture, patting it out about ¾″ deep. Cook in a slow oven, for about 1 hour, until golden-brown. Cool. Remove the paper. Cut into strips about 2″ × ½″.

Mazurka, which is excellent with coffee, will keep for 2–3 weeks in the refrigerator if put in an airtight container.

MIKADA
(*Mikada*)

FOR ABOUT 18 PIECES

2 *tablespoons softened unsalted butter*
2 *eggs*
1 *cup sugar*
1 *cup sour cream*
4 *cups plain flour*
1 *teaspoon baking powder*
1 *cup extra flour for the board*
Boiled Cream Filling (*)

Preheat oven to Reg. 6: 400°. Cream the butter, eggs and sugar together, then add the sour cream. Sieve together the flour and baking-powder and add to mixture, mixing all together. Take a little of the dough and on a very well-floured board roll it out to ⅛″ thickness, either oblong or round. The dough is very sticky and brittle so use plenty of flour. Bake this first layer on a flat baking sheet lined with grease-proof paper until it is light brown, about 10 minutes. Take it from the oven, slide it off the sheet without removing the paper, and chill.

Repeat this process for the next layer, rolling, baking and chilling, and continue until all the dough is used — about 8 or more small layers.

Make a Boiled Cream Filling (*). Let it get cold, then spread it on the first layer of cake, about the same thickness as the cake layer. Repeat this process till all the cake layers and cream are used, finishing with a layer of cream on top.

The cake layers are very brittle so if they start to break up in handling join them together as best you can. The cream filling will stick them together.

SPONGE CAKE WITH BUTTER CREAM

(*Tort Biskvitni s Maslyanim Kremom*)

FOR 12 GENEROUS SLICES

This basic sponge cake may be used for different torts. Either make it in two cake tins, about 8″ in diameter, or in one deep one, cutting it in four layers when cold to add filling.

butter for greasing tins
4 *large or* 6 *small eggs*
1 *cup castor sugar*
1 *cup flour*
2 *teaspoons baking powder*
1½ *tablespoons butter*
4 *tablespoons water*

For Butter Cream
1 *pound unsalted butter*
½ *pound castor sugar*
1 *cup tinned unsweetened evaporated milk*
1 *teaspoon instant coffee* dissolved in 1 *tablespoon hot water*

For moistening cake
1 *teaspoon instant coffee* dissolved in ½ *cup warm water*
1 *tablespoon coffee liqueur*
1 *tablespoon sugar*

Preheat oven to Reg. 3–4: 350°. To make the sponge cake, prepare the cake tins by greasing with butter. Separate the yolks and whites of the eggs. Beat the yolks until well mixed; beat the whites till stiff. Add sugar gradually to the egg whites, beating till the mixture is thick. Add egg yolks and beat till absolutely stiff. Add flour and baking powder sifted together, folding in lightly with an egg whisk. Heat the butter and water together to boiling point and fold in carefully to mixture. Pour into greased tins and bake for 20 minutes .

If there is no time to bake the sponge cake yourself a bought one will do.

To make the butter cream, blend together butter and sugar. Blend in milk gradually, 2 tablespoons at a time, mixing between each addition. When the milk is all in and the butter cream is almost white, add the coffee mixture.

Cut the cake into 4 layers. Moisten the first layer with the coffee-liqueur liquid, then spread the cream over it. Put second layer on top and repeat moistening and spreading. Repeat with each layer. Use two-thirds of the cream for the layers, reserving the rest to cover top and sides and for decoration, using an icing bag.

SPONGE CAKE WITH FRESH CREAM AND PINEAPPLE (*Tort Biskvitni so Slivkami i Ananasom*)

FOR 12 GENEROUS SLICES

1 sponge cake, bought or made as for Sponge Cake with Butter Cream (*)
2 cups fresh cream
1 tablespoon icing sugar
1 1-pound tin pineapple pieces
a few red candied cherries

Strain the liquid from the tinned pineapple. Cut the cake into 4 layers. Whip the cream with the sugar. Moisten the first sponge layer with 2 tablespoons of liquid from the pineapple, then spread on quarter of the cream and put pieces of pineapple on it. Put second layer on top, moisten and spread in same way. Continue till all layers are used, ending with cream and cherries and pineapple pieces arranged in a pattern on the top.

This cake could be made with tinned peaches, strawberries, raspberries, or with fresh fruit. The tinned fruit has a stronger flavour.

WALNUT CAKE
(*Orechovi Tort*)

FOR 12 GENEROUS SLICES

5 eggs
1 cup walnuts
¼ pound butter
½ pound sugar
½ cup milk
2 cups self-raising flour
1 tablespoon breadcrumbs
butter for greasing cake-tin

For Walnut Butter Cream
1 pound unsalted butter
½ pound fine granulated sugar
1 cup unsweetened canned milk
½ cup fine walnut crumbs
½ teaspoon walnut essence
12 walnut halves

Preheat oven to Reg. 3–4: 350°. Separate egg yolks and whites. Grind the walnuts. Cream the butter, sugar and egg yolks together. Add milk and walnuts, mix well and blend in the flour. Beat whites of eggs till stiff then fold into the mixture carefully.

Butter and breadcrumb a 10″ round or square cake-tin, put the mixture into it and bake for 30 minutes. Test by inserting a cake tester and if it comes out sticky leave the cake in the oven for a few more minutes. When cooked, let it stay in the tin for 5 minutes, then put out on a board and cool. The cake should be absolutely cold before putting in the butter cream.

To prepare the Walnut Butter Cream, blend together butter and sugar. Add milk gradually, blending in 2 tablespoons at a time, mixing between each addition. Before adding the flavouring, set aside enough of the white cream for decorating — approximately 1 cup; then add the walnut crumbs and walnut essence to the rest of the mixture. Cut the cold cake into 4 layers and spread the cream on each layer, leaving enough to cover top and sides. Arrange layers one on top of the other. Decorate with the white cream forced through an icing bag and with the walnut halves. Serve with coffee or tea.

MERINGUE CREAM CAKE
(*Tort à la Madame Pavlova*)

FOR 12–15 SERVINGS

1 *cup of egg whites*
2 *cups castor sugar*
2 *cups cream*

Preheat oven to Reg. ½: 200°. Beat the egg whites very stiff, then add the sugar gradually, about 2 tablespoons at a time. Continue beating till all the sugar is used. Drop the mixture from a tablespoon on to a buttered baking-sheet. Cook in a *very* slow oven for at least 2 hours, until the meringues are dried out. Let them cool. This makes about 30 meringues. They can be made any time and kept in an airtight container until needed. (Allow 2 meringues for each person.)

Whip the cream. Spread a thin layer on a plate or serving dish and on it arrange a layer of meringues. Since it is hard to arrange them in layers, put a tablespoon of cream on each meringue and build up the others into a dome-shaped cake. Leave for 1 hour, then serve.

This tort, which is as beautiful and light as Pavlova dancing, has an extravagant Byzantine appearance which adds interest to a party table.

RUM BABA

(*Romavaya Baba*)

FOR 14–16 SERVINGS

Baba has been described as the only true Russian cake; plain baba, baked in a high tin without a central hole, is a traditional Easter cake; yet it is also known to have come from Poland, where it was originally made of rye flour and moistened with sweet Hungarian wine. Baba is made in Turkey and Baba au Rhum is an international menu item. This variation is said to have been invented by King Stanislaus of Poland, who first dipped his kugelhopf into rum. Kugelhopf was made from very early times at Lvov.

2 *ounces fresh (compressed) yeast*
1 *cup lukewarm water*
1 *cup sugar*
1 *cup butter*
4 *eggs*
½ *teaspoon salt*
vanilla, rum, lemon essence to taste
4 *cups flour*
1 *cup sultanas*

For Rum Syrup
1 *cup sugar*
1 *cup water*
¼ *cup rum*

Preheat oven to Reg. 3–4: 350°. Dissolve the yeast in 1 cup of lukewarm water. Blend sugar, butter, eggs together. Add salt and flavouring extracts. Add yeast. Mix well, add flour and beat with a wooden spoon till bubbles start to appear. Add the sultanas. The longer the beating the better and lighter the baba will be.

Cover the mixing bowl with a clean cloth and leave the dough to rise until it has doubled in size. Beat lightly and put into a buttered baba tin about 10″ high, 6″ wide, with a 2″ hollow centre. If you cannot get this traditional baba mould use a 2-pound, fruit or coffee tin with the top cut off neatly.

Baba may also be made in a Turk's Head mould, called in France *moule en couronne*. For such a mould measuring 8″ × 5″, use half the ingredients given here.

Leave the baba to rise in the tin for 30 minutes, then bake in a moderate oven for 25–40 minutes. Test with a long wooden cake tester and if it comes out dry the baba is ready.

Take it from the oven and leave it to cool in the tin for 30–45 minutes; then turn it out carefully. Let it cool completely, for at least 4 hours, before pouring the rum syrup all over, soaking it thoroughly. Traditionally, it is cut into sections from top to bottom, for serving, but these long strips could be cut in halves crossways.

To make the syrup, bring the sugar and water to the boil, add the rum and allow to cool before using.

For a stronger flavour, use rum essence; for variation use Kirsch.

KRENDEL

(*Krendel*)

FOR 20–25 PIECES

This is a sweet, enriched bread which is traditionally made for Name Days, and is also brought to friends' houses when visiting. In appearance it is rather like the Scandinavian Butter Cakes and Continental sweet breads.

1 *ounce fresh (compressed) yeast*
½ *cup warm water*
2 *eggs*
1 *cup sugar*
1 *tablespoon butter*
½ *cup milk*
3½ *cups plain flour*
½ *cup sultanas*
extra flour for pastry board
½ *pound very cold butter*
1 *small egg*
¼ *cup sugar*

Preheat oven to Reg. 3–4: 350°. Melt the yeast in the warm water. Blend eggs, sugar, butter together. Add milk, then yeast, and mix. Add flour and beat well. Add sultanas, mixing them in lightly. Cover the mixing bowl with a cloth and let the dough rise to double its bulk; then put it on a very well-floured board and flatten it with your hand to ¼″ thickness. Slice the cold butter, to ⅛″ thickness, cover half the dough and bring the other half over, covering the butter, then fold in three. Roll out to ½″ thickness and fold in three again. Roll again. Repeat twice. Then roll the dough into a long roll and twist it several times, like a rope. Form it into a big B-shape and put it into a buttered baking dish, about 8″ × 10″, 2″ deep, or on a flat baking sheet. Let it rise again to double its size, then brush with beaten egg and sprinkle top with sugar. Bake for 30–35 minutes. Test with a wooden cake tester and if it comes out dry the krendel is cooked.

Take it out of the oven and leave it on baking sheet for 10 minutes, then put it on a rack and let it cool before cutting into sections.

Marinated Fruit and Vegetables. Sauces (Marinovaniye Frukti i Ovoschi. Sousa)

Marinated Fruit (Marinovaniye Frukti)

Originally used to preserve fruit and vegetables out of season and supply a source of winter vitamin foods, marinades are also eaten for their fresh and pleasant taste, as an accompaniment to meat and to freshen the palate during a large meal. They go very well with shaslik or poultry.

In Russia, oak leaves are sometimes put into dill pickles to make them firm and blackcurrant leaves are added to give a pleasant scent.

MARINADE FOR FRUIT

The following marinade is used for apples, pears, quinces, grapes and cherries. If the jars are kept in a cool place or in the refrigerator they will last for months.

5 *cups water*
2 *teaspoons cloves*
½ *teaspoon peppercorns*
5–6 *bay leaves*
3 *cups sugar*
½ *stick cinnamon*
1½ *ounces acetic acid*, 33⅓% *strength* (*or white vinegar*)

Boil all the ingredients together for 5 minutes. Chill. Take out the cinnamon stick before pouring marinade over the fruit.

This amount of marinade is enough for a ½ gallon jar of fruit.

TO PREPARE APPLES AND PEARS FOR MARINADE

Wash the fruit. Put it in cold water. Bring to the boil and cook for 3 minutes. Watch the fruit so that the skin does not crack. Take out of boiling water, leaving fruit whole or cut in halves. Pour the marinade over and leave for 2 days.

TO PREPARE QUINCES

Peel and cut into long pieces. Boil until soft. Strain well. Pour marinade over.

TO PREPARE CHERRIES AND GRAPES

Make the marinade. Bring it to the boil. Drop in the washed fruit and remove from heat. Chill, then pour into jars. May be eaten in a day or two.

Marinated Vegetables (Marinovaniye Ovoschi)

MARINATED BEETROOT (*Marinovanaya Svekla*)

Make the marinade as for Marinated Fruit (*), using 1 cup instead of 3 cups of sugar. Cook the beetroot, until soft, then remove skins. (Be careful not to overcook.) Put them in a jar and pour the marinade over. The same recipe is used for Pumpkin.

BUTTON MUSHROOMS OR MUSHROOM STALKS (*Marinovaniye Gribi*)

10 *cups water*
juice of 1 *lemon*
2 *pounds mushrooms or mushroom stalks*
marinade as for Marinated Fruit (*) *using* 1 *cup instead of* 3 *cups of sugar*

If using mushroom stalks, cut them in ½″ sections. Button mushrooms are left whole.

Heat up the water and when boiling add the lemon juice and the mushrooms or stalks. Boil for 2–3 minutes, then take out the mushrooms with a perforated spoon and put them immediately into cold water. This makes them crisp. Let them cool, then put mushrooms into a colander, pressing slightly to extract excess water. Put into a jar and pour marinade over.

MARINATED CABBAGE
(*Marinovanaya Kapusta*)

For marinade

1 cup vinegar
3 cups water
1 cup sugar
3 bay leaves
a few peppercorns and cloves

2 pounds cabbage
1 tablespoon salt

Boil the marinade ingredients together and chill. Shred the cabbage very thin, sprinkle it with salt and mix well on a board, lightly rubbing in the salt. Put into a glass jar, pour the marinade over and leave in the refrigerator for 2–3 days. Serve with cold meat, shaslik or as a zakuska.

LIGHTLY-SALTED CUCUMBER
(*Malosolniye Ogurtzi*)

These are salted, not preserved, and will only keep for a week to ten days. For longer preservation a different method, given below, is used.

10 young cucumbers, about 5"–6" long
1 large sprig of dill
3–4 cloves garlic
bay leaf
peppercorns
12 cups water
2 tablespoons salt

Slice both ends off young cucumbers and slit the skins lengthways in about 6 to 8 places.

Put them into a heat-proof container. Add the dill — stalk and leaves — garlic, bay leaf and peppercorns. Boil the water with the salt and pour over the cucumbers. They should be well covered. They will float but push them down, packing them in securely, if necessary putting a weight on top. They will be ready to eat next day. They will keep a week or ten days in the refrigerator.

SALTED CUCUMBER
(Soleniye Ogurtzi)

For salting liquid

12 cups water
6 tablespoons salt
2¼ cups vinegar
10 young cucumbers, about 5" long, approximately the same shape
1 large sprig of dill
a few peppercorns
3–4 cloves garlic
a few mustard seeds
1 horseradish root
10–15 oak leaves (if obtainable)

Boil together the water, salt and vinegar. Let it cool thoroughly.

Wash the cucumbers. On the bottom of a large earthenware jar put a layer of dill, peppercorns, garlic, mustard seed, horseradish and an oak leaf. On top tightly pack a row of cucumbers. Put in another layer of seasonings, then more cucumbers, making as many layers as you need and ending with the seasonings. Put a weighted board on top and pour the cold salted water over the cucumbers. Keep in a cool storage room for 25–30 days, until matured. They will last for several months if kept cool.

DILL PICKLED CUCUMBERS
(Marinovaniye Ogurtzi)

These are very popular in Russia, not only because cucumbers grow so freely but because they provide vitamins during winter months when fresh vegetables are scarce.

Choose small cucumbers, no more than 2"–2½" long.

For marinade

5 cups water
1 ounce acetic acid, 33⅓% strength
½ teaspoon cloves
1 teaspoon peppercorns
4–5 bay leaves
1½ teaspoons salt
1½ teaspoons sugar

3 dozen small cucumbers
a saucepan of boiling water
large sprig of dill

Boil the marinade ingredients together and chill. Wash the cucumbers, put them in a sieve or colander and submerge them in a saucepan of fast-boiling water for 3–5 seconds. Lift out and immediately put into cold water. This makes them crisp and preserves their natural colour.

Put the cucumbers into a glass jar in layers with dill between each layer. Pour the marinade over. Leave for 5–6 days. They will keep for 4 or 5 months in a cool storage room, or may be eaten at once.

Sauces (Sous)

Many of the sauces used in Russian cooking are direct imports from France and are found in any general cook book. Those given here are more typically Russian.

HORSERADISH
(*Hren*)

FOR 1½ CUPS

½ pound grated horseradish
1 *tablespoon white wine vinegar*
salt to taste

Thoroughly clean the horseradish roots, then grate on a fine grater. Mix in with vinegar and add salt to taste.

HORSERADISH WITH BEET
(*Hren so Svekloi*)

FOR ¾ CUP

½ *cup ready-made horseradish* (*)
¼ *cup Marinated Beetroot* (*) *finely chopped*

Mix together thoroughly.

HORSERADISH AND SOUR-CREAM SAUCE
(*Hren so Smetanoi*)

FOR 1½ CUPS

1 *cup ready-made horseradish* (*)
½ *cup sour cream*

Mix together thoroughly. This is much milder than ordinary horseradish.

MUSTARD
(*Gorchitza*)
FOR 1 CUP

½ cup mustard powder
½ cup sugar
1 teaspoon salt
a little boiling water
juice of ½ a lemon

Mix together the mustard, sugar and salt, adding enough boiling water to moisten. Add the lemon juice and mix again.

GRAVY FOR MEAT OR POULTRY
(*Sousa Myasnoï*)

After roasting meat or poultry, strain off excess fat from the pan, heat up the remaining juices and add 2 tablespoons of sour cream. Stir in well, boil up and serve in a sauce-boat.

MAYONNAISE
(*Mayanez* or *Provençal*)
FOR 2 CUPS

2 egg yolks
1½ cups oil
1 teaspoon salt
1½ teaspoons sugar
juice of ½ a lemon

Put the raw yolks in a mixing bowl. Stir, adding oil, a few drops at a time, until almost all is used. Add salt, sugar, lemon juice and continue to stir, adding the rest of the oil.

WHITE SAUCE
(*Beli Sous*)
FOR 3 CUPS

3 tablespoons butter
2 tablespoons flour
2 cups milk
½ cup sour (or fresh) cream
salt and pepper
chopped dill

Melt the butter, add the flour and stir until blended. Add the milk slowly, stirring all the time to avoid lumps. Draw the saucepan off the fire when adding milk. Cook slowly for about 10 minutes. Add the sour cream (or fresh cream if preferred), salt and pepper. When serving, sprinkle with chopped dill.

SOUR CREAM AND MUSHROOM SAUCE

(*Smetani Sous s Gribami*)

FOR 3 CUPS

1 *cup chopped onion*
2 *tablespoons butter*
½ *pound sliced mushrooms*
½ *teaspoon salt*
pepper
1½ *cups sour cream*

Fry onion in butter. Add the sliced mushrooms. Season. Fry together for 5–10 minutes. Add sour cream and bring to the boil.

Special Occasions

The Russian love of gaiety turns traditional feasts and celebrations into lively affairs. The beginning of Lent, Easter and Christmas, family birthdays and Name Days (Imenini), are always good for a party, and weddings, christenings, anniversaries and picnics help to fill up the year.

Nina's household celebrates every possible occasion and the parties are always good. If there are a great many people the supper or dinner is *à la fourchette*, but she would rather have us round a long table, which she claims is better for toasts, a vital part of Russian gatherings. Though she prepares everything herself she still manages to enjoy the party.

Her method is simple. For very big parties she has cold food and it is all set out on the table . . . sliced poultry and hams, fish and aspics, brawns and salads of all kinds, with compôtes of marinaded fruits spaced out between. Everyone helps themselves or each other, which means that Nina can preside at the table instead of spending a hot resentful evening in the kitchen.

Toasting is constant and enthusiastic — the guest of honour, the patron saint, Fair Ladies, the host and hostess, absent friends, the guests, together and in turn. If there is a lull in the drinking or if the party seems to be falling into sections — people talking too exclusively to neighbours — there are drinking songs to bring them all together again.

One of these songs is a simple affair in which A fills B's glass, while the company sings, and when B has emptied the glass he fills C's and so on round the table, the bottle passing from hand to hand. Another song starts: 'All those born in January, stand up, stand up and drink.' When they have done so the chorus goes on to February, and so through each month of the year. When December is reached people are usually in the mood to return to January and repeat it all again.

A song called *Charichka*, The Silver Cup, is slightly more elaborate. A glass is presented ceremoniously to one of the guests with an invocation, sung as a solo: 'Here is a silver cup on a golden tray. . . . Whoever drinks from it will have good health. Drink and enjoy good fortune, our dear Nina Konstantinovna — or Mikhail Nikolayevich or Pavel Andrianovich . . .' etc., etc.

The honoured one takes the glass and empties it while the company sings, 'Drink it up! Drink it up!' And then, 'She has drunk it, she has drunk it. *Na zdarovya*! Good Health!' at which they also empty their glasses.

Pancake Day (Maslyanitza)

Seven weeks before Easter Nina holds a blini party. This is to mark the approach of the Great Fast (Lent) which continues till midnight on Easter Saturday.

The date of the Russian Easter varies but is usually a few weeks later than in the western church. From time to time the two Easters coincide.

During the Great Fast strict Orthodox Russians eat nothing but vegetables and vegetable oils, which is severe discipline for a healthy Russian appetite, but people can break themselves in gradually through the Butter Fast or Little Fast, which lasts for a week before the Great Fast. During this week they may eat fish and dairy products but no meat.

Gastronomically speaking, the most important outcome of this Butter Fast was the invention of blini or pancakes. These are said to descend from a pagan spring rite, taken over by the Christian missionaries who converted Russia, and that each blin or pancake symbolises the sun, welcomed back after the winter darkness.

Blini are smaller and thicker than western pancakes and may be of wheat, rye or buckwheat flour. Their main difference is that they are made with yeast, which gives a wonderful lightness. In the old days in Russia, and still in country districts, heavy cast-iron frying-pans were kept specially and used for nothing else. Sometimes they were shaped like a clover leaf to take three pancakes at the same time, or with two round 'leaves'. Blini can be made very successfully with an ordinary frying-pan on top of the stove or with an electric frying-pan at the table. Do not be discouraged if your first efforts are not successful. The Russians have a saying, 'Pervi blin komon'. 'The first pancake is always a lump.'

Blini may be eaten at any time during the Little Fast and as often as you like, but most people have one big pancake party towards the end of the week, usually the Sunday before the Great Fast begins.

These parties are not at all like the western Pancake Day. The blini are eaten with caviar, anchovies, herrings, salted salmon, any kind of fish and served with plenty of sour cream and melted butter.

There are no zakuski and at Nina's the procedure is simple. The fish, sour cream and butter are set on the dining-room table where the guests sit waiting. In the kitchen Nina ladles out spoonfuls from an immense pot of bubbling liquid dough, pours them into a hot buttered frying-pan and as the blini are cooked, piles them on a plate and sends them to the table where they are seized by the guests, spread with fish, drenched with smetana (sour cream) and washed down with vodka. Even those who have no intention of keeping the Great Fast eat and drink as though this were their last chance.

In the early stages of the party each pile of blini coming from the kitchen is greeted with eager cries and quickly demolished, but as time passes and the toasts become more frequent, as the voices rise and the caviar and salmon disappear, consumption slows down until at last saturation point is reached.

Vodka is a help in neutralizing the cream and fats and is the only drink possible with such a meal. For a pancake party, work on the basis that 1 cup of liquid, milk and water combined, makes enough pancakes for 1 person.

RUSSIAN PANCAKES
(*Blini*)

3 *eggs*
1 *ounce fresh (compressed) yeast*
1½ *cups luke-warm water*
1 *teaspoon salt*
1 *tablespoon sugar*
2–2½ *cups plain flour*
2 *cups milk*
butter for frying

Separate the egg yolks and whites. Dissolve the yeast in ¼ cup warm water. Add the rest of the water, egg yolks, salt and sugar. Mix well together, add the flour and beat thoroughly.

Beat the egg whites stiff, add to the mixture, folding in carefully, and allow to rise until it doubles itself in bulk, about 2–2½ hours.

Boil the milk and pour it into the dough while still boiling hot. Mix fast and well. Cover the mixing-bowl and allow dough to rise for one hour, without touching it. It should become full of small bubbles. Do not mix or stir before cooking.

Heat a frying-pan and brush it with melted butter, or just put in half a teaspoon of butter. Using a ladle, carefully scoop out about half a cup of dough. It should be taken from round the edges of the bowl so that the rest of the mixture is not disturbed. Pour it from the ladle into the frying-pan and cook on one side until the top is almost completely done; then put a small piece of butter in the centre of the pancake, turn it over and cook for a few more minutes. Remove to an oven-proof plate and keep hot in the oven while you make the next blin. Repeat the process until all the dough is cooked, piling the pancakes one upon the other.

Easter (Paskha)

At the end of the Great Fast comes Easter, the biggest festival in the Russian year, even more important than Christmas. It has been described by many Russian writers, and émigrés all over the world celebrate it, even in countries where Easter marks the beginning of Autumn instead of Spring.

Nina and her friends always observed it in the traditional way, with an Easter breakfast after midnight mass at the Orthodox Cathedral. Since the festivities go on all night, those who do not have to be at church early to sing in the choir or perform some other service usually have a sleep beforehand. By eleven o'clock the cathedral and its grounds are crowded with waiting people, all holding candles. Some talk quietly, others are silent, their faces sad, their thoughts far away. The atmosphere is subdued, the voices lowered. It is a beautiful and moving scene . . . the clear night with its sparkling stars, the wavering flames of candles shining up into the pale faces, faces that matured and aged in China, in Australia, in different parts of Europe; prosperous, poor, old, young, handsome, decrepit, well-born, humble . . . all united in their common blood and in this festival.

As the hours pass the crowd increases and by midnight the surrounding streets are filled with parked cars. At the doors of the cathedral a steady stream makes its way in and out of the building. Inside, the altar and ikons blaze with candles. The heat is stifling. Men and women in their best clothes, children, old babushkas in shawls and kerchiefs, all carrying candles, press slowly towards the centre of the church where the ikon of the dead Christ is lying, bend down and kiss it, then push their way out again, stopping to greet friends or halted by the density of the crowd.

On the last moments of Easter Saturday the ikon of Christ is carried behind the altar screen; then at midnight the gates are opened and the bishops and priests come out, dressed in white. With acolytes swinging censers, followed by the singing choir and the worshippers with their candles, the bishops, priests and deacons file out of the church. The procession circles the building, stopping at each of the four corners, north, south, east and west, then back to the entrance.

'*Khristos Voskrese!* Christ is risen!'

The censers are swung. The incense rises.

'*Khristos Voskrese! Khristos Voskrese!*'

Mourning is over. Christ is risen. The cry goes up all round. Everyone turns to his or her neighbour, no matter whom, saying, 'Christ is risen!' 'Vo istinu voskres!' ('He is risen indeed!') the neighbour replies and they kiss three times, on the right cheek, left cheek and right again.

The procession re-enters the church but now the crowd begins to disperse. People move off to their cars, on foot, in groups. There is a change of mood, of tempo. Voices ring out, car engines start up and soon the great gathering has melted away, gone to their own or to friends' houses for the Easter breakfast. For the really strict Orthodox Russian this breaks the fast which began on Pancake Day, but even those who have denied themselves nothing during Lent are eager for the meal, for one goes to the service on an empty stomach.

At Nina's house the feast lasts for thirty-six hours, in shifts, the first session starting immediately after church, about one o'clock, the second a late lunch on Easter Sunday, for there is open house all day. On the table are all the foods forbidden during Lent — hams and poultry, many zakuski, brawns and aspics. There is less fish than usual, since people are rather tired of it by the end of Lent, and piles of brightly-painted hard-boiled eggs are arranged on stands among the dishes. Everyone takes one of these Easter eggs and laughingly cracks the shell by knocking it against their neighbour's egg. Since the decorations are done with food colouring the eggs may be eaten with the zakuski.

The main features of the Easter table are the traditional kulichi and paskha, which émigré Russians continued to make during the years when church festivals were no longer celebrated in their native land. There is no recipe for either kulich or paskha in some of the modern Soviet cookery books but the older émigré housewives have passed them on to the younger generation. Nina, whose paskha is famous, is usually stopped as she comes out of church in the last week of Lent and asked for her recipe.

Good paskha is smooth, light and fine, a pyramid of cream cheese impregnated with dried fruits and nuts. Beside it on the table are the kulichi, domed cylinders of rich sweet bread with fruit, standing upright like little Byzantine towers. To eat kulich the top is cut off and slices taken from the middle, then the top put back to prevent dryness, for it stays on the table long after Easter — traditionally for forty days, until Ascension.

Easter breakfasts are the best of all Russian parties. There is an air of excitement in starting at one o'clock in the morning and in the contrast between the subdued waiting at the church and the sense of happiness and liberation that follows; for though someone is sure to lapse into a Dostoevsky mood sooner or later the atmosphere is joyful. No one seeing these people so wholeheartedly enjoying themselves would guess that next day some of them, no longer young, will be working at machines in factories or at menial jobs in hospitals, living a hard and circumscribed life until the next time there is a party.

EASTER MENU

Since Nina always goes to church on Easter night she does her preparations for the party beforehand. The whole meal is cold, so hams and poultry may be cooked in advance. The paskha and kulichi are made a couple of days ahead and the Easter eggs hard-boiled and painted with food colouring. (We suggest allowing 8 dozen eggs for the party, for decorated eggs, zakuski, cakes, kulichi and paskha.)

A suggested menu for about 10 people could include:

Zakuski: Sprats
Smoked Eel (*)
Anchovies
Marinaded Fish in Tomato Sauce
Decorated Hard-boiled Eggs

Meat: Home-made Ham (*)
Roast Duck (or Goose) with Apples (*)
Chicken and Vegetable Salad (*)
Brawn (*)

Sweets: *Paskha* (*)
Kulich (*)
Tort à la Madame Pavlova (*)
Marinated Fruits (*)

Drinks: Vodka
Zubrowka
Wine
Cognac
Liqueurs
Coffee
Russian Tea

KULICH

Kulich is a tall cylindrical loaf with a domed top and stands upright on its base. It can be baked successfully in a 2-pound dried-milk or coffee tin with the top cut off smoothly. For a specially big kulich use an 8-pound tin; for very small loaves, the 1-pound size.

This quantity of dough will fill 4 2-pound tins

3 *ounces fresh (compressed) yeast*
1 *cup warm water*
2½ *cups milk*
1½ *pounds sugar*
1½ *teaspoons salt*
4 *pounds plain flour*
12–15 *egg yolks (depending on size)*
2 *vanilla beans or vanilla essence to taste*
½ *teaspoon nutmeg*
few drops lemon essence
1 *pound sultanas*
½ *pound diced glacé pineapple or cherries*
¼ *pound candied orange peel*
½ *pound chopped almonds*
1 *pound butter*
fine breadcrumbs for cake-tin

Preheat oven to Reg. ½–1: 250°. Dissolve the yeast in 1 cup of warm water. Slightly warm the milk, put it into a bowl, add ½-pound of the sugar, the salt and yeast. Add 1½ pounds of the flour, beat well with a wooden spoon and leave to rise. In the meantime blend the rest of the sugar and egg yolks together, add the lemon essence, vanilla and nutmeg. If using vanilla beans, scrape out the centre with a spoon or knife and mix in thoroughly with a little sugar.

Prepare the fruit and almonds. When the dough has doubled itself in size, melt the butter but do not overheat — just warm it. Add it to the dough, mix it in, then add the sugar and egg-yolk mixture. Mix again. Add half the remaining flour. Mix. Add the rest of the flour. The dough should now be quite firm, too firm to mix with a spoon so work with your hand or even clenched fist, pushing and pummelling it for as long as you like — the longer the better. It should not stick to the hand at all when it is ready.

Add the fruit and nuts, working them in carefully so they do not break up. Cover with a clean cloth and stand in a warm place, out of draughts, until the dough doubles itself in size. (2–3 hours.)

Butter the 2-pound tins and sprinkle them with fine bread-crumbs. When the dough has risen, fill one-third of each tin, leaving room for rising. Stand for 30 minutes.

Bake in a slow oven for 1½–2 hours, at most, until a long wooden cake tester comes out dry. The tin must stand on its base in the oven.

Cover a soft pillow with grease-proof paper. Take the kulich from the oven and leave it in its tin for 10 minutes; then slide it out carefully on its side on the pillow. Roll it gently from side to side every few minutes to preserve its shape. If left too long on one side it will lose its roundness. Do not try to stand it up until it is completely cool.

To serve, cut off the top, take slices from the kulich, then put the top back to prevent dryness.

PASKHA

FOR 8–10 SERVINGS

Many countries have cream cheese sweets and desserts; there are Italian ricotta recipes, French hot and cold cream cheese creations, German and Austrian cheese cakes. It is possible that Russian paskha derives from one of these but it far surpasses them all.

For a really good paskha only the very best of materials should be used and there must be no skimping. It is rather an extravagant recipe but since it is usually made only once a year Russian housewives do not try to economise, for when it is well made it must be one of the most delicious sweets ever invented.

It is made with or without cooking; without fruit; with almonds only; with fruit and no almonds; or with both fruit and almonds. Uncooked paskha is far softer and finer than the cooked version.

1 *pound fresh unsalted cream cheese, not too moist*
½ *pound unsalted butter*
½ *pound castor sugar*
4 *egg yolks*
vanilla essence to taste
1 *pound mixed chopped sultanas, glacé pineapple, cherries, angelica and almonds*

Put the cream cheese through a very fine sieve. In another bowl, cream the butter, sugar and egg yolks together until all the sugar has dissolved. Add vanilla essence and, gradually, the cream cheese. Mix well, add fruit and almonds and mix them in lightly.

If you have a pyramid paskha-mould line it with a damp cloth, leaving enough cloth to cover the top. Put in the mixture, cover with the cloth and a small board and put a 2-pound weight to press on it for 24 hours. When ready, unmould on to a dish or compôte, with the pointed side up, and serve.

If there is no pyramid mould, use a colander lined with a damp cloth or a large clean lined flower-pot, also covered and weighted. Do not use ordinary basins for if the pressed-out moisture cannot escape the paskha will be soggy and start to separate.

A colander gives a round pascha, a flower-pot gives a slightly chimney-shaped one; but if you want the traditional shape and cannot get the wooden mould with detachable sides, form into a pyramid with a knife, after removing from colander or flower pot.

COOKED PASKHA

(*Paskha Varyonaya*)

FOR 8–10 SERVINGS

2 *pounds unsalted fresh cream cheese*
6 *egg yolks*
1 *pound sugar*
1 *pound unsalted butter*
vanilla essence to taste
1 *cup sour cream*
½ *pound chopped almonds*

Wrap the cream cheese in a cloth and put it between two boards with a weight on top for 6–8 hours; then put it through a fine sieve.

Cream the yolks, sugar and butter, add the vanilla essence, then the sour cream. Mix in with the cream cheese. Add the almonds. Put into a double saucepan, heat almost to boiling point but do not boil. Let it cool, put into a mould lined with a clean damp cloth, cover and set under a 2-pound weight for 24 hours.

Christmas (Rozhdestvo)

By comparison with Easter, the Russian Christmas is a quiet affair, mainly devoted to children and family and not celebrated in the lavish way that greets the end of Lent. It is held later than in the western church, on the 7th January, and strict Orthodox Russians fast for six weeks beforehand. This is a completely vegetarian fast and while it lasts there must be no parties or gay gatherings. It is broken on Christmas Eve, when the first star appears, with a traditional dish called Kutya. After this the tree is decorated; then, on Christmas Day, the table is set for the family dinner.

A typical Christmas menu includes Goose with Apples (*), duck, ham, preceded by many zakuski. The sweets are usually cookies called Hvorost (Branches) (*); fruit cake called Mazurka (*), nuts and dried fruits, sweets and some kind of tort, served with coffee or tea.

During Christmas no one need wait for an invitation to visit friends and people drop in on each other throughout the holiday, to drink tea and exchange greetings.

Kutya, with which the fast is broken, is made in different ways in different parts of Russia. In the south it is made with boiled rice and raisins, honey and walnuts; in Central Russia, with cooked whole wheat, honey, poppy-seed, sultanas and walnuts. The same mixture is also served at Orthodox funerals when it is dealt out to the mourners from a great dish. It is an ancient Slavonic custom.

KUTYA

FOR 4 SERVINGS

1 cup hot boiled rice
½ cup sugar
1 tablespoon honey
½ cup raisins

When the water has been drained off the boiled rice, mix in the sugar and honey. Turn on to a serving-dish and scatter raisins on top. This makes about 2 cups of Kutya.

Imenini (Name Day)

All Orthodox Russians are christened after saints. The only names permitted to them are listed in a book kept by the priest.

This means that as well as having a birthday to celebrate they also have a name day or patron saint's day. This is a more important occasion than a birthday because it is also a religious holy day. Strict Orthodox believers go to church before their party to honour their saint. Others content themselves with the party. Due to the number of saints in the Russian calendar, Imenini parties seem to occur with great frequency.

These parties are often very elaborate, with many rich dishes, but the old traditional Imenini food was a pirog or pie. Pirog is still included in all Name Day menus and may contain meat, fish, cabbage or other fillings. It could even be like the pirog described by Gogol, which had four corners, each with a different filling — one containing a sturgeon's cheeks, another mushrooms, onions and kasha and so on. At Imenini parties the pirog is preceded by zakuski and the first three toasts are always drunk to the guest of honour whose name-day is being celebrated.

Though modern Imenini parties are usually organised, with people invited in advance, the old custom was to keep open house, when anyone could drop in for a piece of pie or krendel (*), a special sweet loaf, or a cup of tea. Sometimes the callers started to arrive in the morning and the visits went on all day. In this, as in all traditional Russian customs, the emphasis is on hospitality, on opening one's house to friends and strangers, on sharing one's food, drink, gaiety and good fellowship.

Weddings (Sva'dba)

The first experience of a Russian wedding is very impressive. It is quite unfamiliar in many ways, not only in the spectacular ceremony and magnificent singing but in the fact that it is likely to be held on a Sunday and that the congregation remain standing for the whole of the service.

In pagan Russia, among certain tribes, the bridegroom had to kidnap his bride; in others he had to pay the clan for her. Later, this payment was replaced by a gift from the bridegroom to the bride or her parents.

After Christianity came, engagements and weddings were blessed by the church but at first this custom was only observed by princes and *boyars* — hereditary noblemen. Up till the fifteenth century the people, specially in country districts, required only official recognition of the marriage by the clan or community.

Under Byzantine law marriages could take place at an early age. In the eighth century it was 15 for men, 13 for women; in the 9th century it was 14 for men and 12 for women.

Until a couple of generations ago parents made the matches and arranged the marriages and there are still Russian women living who were married in this way, some of them never having seen their bridegrooms before the ceremony. This often happened when the couple lived in different districts.

Though Russian life has changed so much certain customs survive and many young émigrés follow the traditional procedure. The engagement is not announced with a ring and photographs in the paper but an agreement is made between the families, and though the parents do not make the choice, their blessing is asked. This is given before an ikon, the young pair kneeling before the parents.

Three or four weeks before the ceremony the marriage is announced in church, then, one week before, the engaged pair take communion together. They do not meet for 24 hours before they arrive at the church on the wedding day. The bridegroom should not see the wedding dress.

The bride comes to the church with her veil over her face and is met by the priest and bridegroom. In a short service their engagement is publicly confirmed. This may be done any time during the engagement but is usual just before the wedding. The bride stands on the left, the bridegeroom on the right. The priest joins their hands together and offers up a special prayer for them; then the bride's veil is put back and the party moves into the centre of the church for the main ceremony.

This is beautiful, bizarre and fascinating, with superb music and singing. The priest gives both bride and groom a lighted candle to hold during the service. Rings are exchanged three times; the sacramental wine is sipped and finally the priest leads the couple three times round the centre of the church.

During the ceremony the groomsmen, taking turns, hold heavy crowns over the heads of bride and groom.

There are no pews in a Russian church and the friends and relations stand round on both sides, many in tears. The parents are not present. They wait at the reception to greet the bride and groom with an ikon and the traditional bread and salt or Happiness Cake.

One mother offers the bread and salt — a little round loaf with a small salt-cellar in the top, and the other, holding an ikon, blesses and welcomes the newlyweds. After the blessing, the bread and salt are tasted. This is symbolic of cleaning away past sins, of starting a fresh life together, of health and happiness.

Before the guests sit down to the wedding breakfast there is a champagne toast to the married couple and then the party gets under way. The long table is covered with food and drink. Unlike our traditional mixture of fruit and spirits the wedding cake is an immense sweet affair which the bride and groom cut together and pass round. None is taken home to sleep on or posted off to absent friends. Every scrap is demolished on the spot.

The banquet is long and hilarious. There are no speeches but endless toasts and constant cries of '*Gorko! Gorko!*' ('Bitter') from the guests. This means that the food is bitter and the bride and groom must kiss to make it sweeter.

The length of the ceremony and the fact that everyone stands up through it does not dampen enthusiasm. It only increases appetite.

The newlyweds are not expected to go early and often stay till the end of the party. Before leaving, the bride throws her flowers to her bridesmaids and there is a noisy farewell. If there is still food and drink on the table the guests return to it after the departure and carry on till all is finished.

WEDDING CAKE

There is no special recipe for wedding cake. It is just any rich sweet cake or tort such as are given in the cake chapter of this book.

HAPPINESS CAKE

(*Bread and Salt — Hleb s Sol'yu*)

6 *ounces butter*	1 *ounce fresh (compressed) yeast*
4 *tablespoons sugar*	¼ *cup water*
1 *teaspoon salt*	1 *pound plain flour*
vanilla essence to taste	*a little nutmeg*
1 *cup milk*	*butter and breadcrumbs for baking tin*

Preheat the oven to Reg. 3–4: 350°. Cream the softened butter with the sugar and add the salt, eggs, vanilla, then the milk. Dissolve the yeast in ¼ cup warm water and add to mixture. With a wooden spoon beat in the flour and nutmeg, beating the dough for 5–10 minutes. Leave it to rise. Butter and breadcrumb a round baking-tin, not too deep. When the dough has doubled itself in bulk put it carefully into the tin and leave for 10–15 minutes. Brush it with beaten egg and bake in a moderate oven for 30–35 minutes, till a testing straw comes out clean.

When cooked, leave for 10 minutes in the tin, then remove and cool on a rack.

On the wedding day put in the top of the cake a little container to hold the salt.

This cake is used to welcome loved and respected friends arriving to stay. Bread and salt are old symbols of respect or allegiance, as in the Russian epic of *Sadko, The Rich Merchant of Novgorod:*

To the Tsar beyond the sea
I have never paid tribute or duty . . .
And in the blue Khvalinsk sea
I never threw bread and salt.

Picnics (Picnics)

There is something stimulating about a Russian picnic. No time is wasted on long hot drives; the nearest, shadiest, prettiest place is chosen and quickly strewn with cushions, rugs, umbrellas, bottles of vodka, jars of shaslik, skewers, baskets of zakuski, salads, pirogs and torts. The quiet country air is shattered with exuberant cries, Russian songs, the sound of axes, shouts and arguments about the best place to build the fire. The first thing is to find somewhere to keep the vodka cool, preferably a stream or pool; then all must have a drink and a snack to revive them after the journey. The axe-man, fire builders, cook and onlookers must be fortified. Zakuski are unpacked; the meat and onions for shaslik taken from their marinade and threaded on the skewers. It is thirsty work and another round of vodka is needed; then another, while you wait for the fire to burn down to the right state for cooking shaslik. The feast, when it finally starts, is long and varied and followed by somnolence, arguments, declaiming of poems and songs.

Shaslik, the great picnic food, is the Caucasian name for cooking on skewers. It is very similar to Turkish and Persian şiş kebab and the Greek souvlakia but the meat is cut into bigger pieces and the skewers are larger. The Caucasians use their swords. Each country claims to have invented this wonderful way of cooking meat — the Turks say the Greeks took it from them, the Russians say the Turks took it from the Caucasians, the Greeks say it was theirs to start with. In the Iliad, Homer describes the Greeks cooking pieces of lamb on skewers outside the walls of Troy; yet Troy is in Asia Minor (Turkey) and the Turks came from the land of Touran, beyond the Caucasus and the Caspian Sea. Whoever invented it, it is a masterpiece; and though it is now served in restaurants all over the world the best way is to eat it is out of doors, with plenty of red wine, surrounded by the scents of charcoal smoke and cooking lamb.

Shaslik varies in different regions of Russia. Abkhasian shaslik is made of fat mutton and sheep's liver cut into pieces; Georgian shaslik of meat and onion, without liver; Uzbekistan shaslik is cooked on wooden skewers instead of metal; Baku shaslik is of lamb or mutton cut into one-ounce pieces. Normally the meat is marinated in lemon juice but in southern Russia pomegranate juice is used. This custom could have come from Persia, where pomegranate juice is used for this and other dishes.

LAMB COOKED ON SKEWERS
(*Shaslik*)

a 7-pound leg of lamb
salt and pepper
Optional
1 *pound bacon*

1½ *pounds onions*
juice of 6–7 *lemons, depending on size*

The night before the picnic, remove all the fat and bones from the meat and cut it into pieces about 2″ square by ½″ thick. Salt and pepper and put into a big jar of glass or earthenware or anything that is not affected by the acid of lemon juice. Slice the onions and put them in the jar between layers of the meat. Pour the lemon juice over it all and leave all night. The jar should be full of alternate layers of onion and meat.

Tomatoes cut in quarters, strips of green peppers and sections of bacon are sometimes added at the last minute, not marinaded overnight with the meat. To prepare for cooking, thread meat, bacon, onion, peppers, tomatoes alternately on the skewers till each one is full.

Cook over hot charcoal or glowing embers, turning the skewers so the meat cooks evenly on all sides.

Marinated fruit go well with shaslik, which is really a meal in itself, but Russian picnics being what they are there will probably be many zakuski, mainly tinned and smoked fish, salame and other sausages, all easy to transport. All sorts of pirogs and piroshki, breads and torts are popular picnic foods and Forshmak in Kalach (*), a cold meat and herring mixture in a horseshoe loaf. Potato salad, cold pot-roast (*) and cold Home-made Ham (*) may be included and the drinks are usually vodka, brandy and red wine.

Shaslik could be cooked on a stove, under the grill, though it would lack the flavour that comes from cooking over charcoal in the open air.

Russian Drinks
(Russkiye Napitki)

'Drinking is the joy of the Rus. He cannot exist without that pleasure,' said St Vladimir, explaining to the Moslem emissaries why his country could not embrace Islam, which prohibits alcohol.

Love of strong drink and ability to take large amounts of it is a Russian characteristic that has often astonished foreigners. Brillat-Savarin once remarked that 'the ration of a sick Russian, in 1815, would have made a strong porter of the Paris markets drunk.'

Most non-Russians regard vodka as Russia's national drink; yet this much-loved spirit is comparatively modern. In ancient times, even the Kievan period, when Kiev was capital, there was no distilled liquor. It was not till the fourteenth century that the Russians learnt the art of distilling from grain, from Genoans living in the Crimea.

The oldest traditional Slav drinks are kvass and med (mead). They are both mentioned in an early fifth-century account of a Byzantine envoy travelling across Russia from Constantinople to visit Attila, the Hun, but appear to date from much earlier.

Mead was very popular in Kievan Russia and was drunk freely by both monks and laymen. The ancient chronicles describe St Vladimir ordering three hundred kettles of mead for the opening of a new church, and mention a twelfth-century prince who kept five hundred casks of mead in his cellar.

Mead is fermented honey and never lost its popularity with the Russians. Nineteenth-century travellers describe mead sold at railway stations in old Dutch or German silver beakers. There were several varieties, sweet, dry or peppered. Modern Russians are fond of a rather similar drink called Brajka, made from fermented wheat and honey.

Beer (Pivo) has been drunk in Russia for many centuries and in early days was considered part of the basic diet. St Sergius of Radonezh, subjecting himself to mortification and prayer in his cell near Moscow, is said to have fasted so severely that 'he denied himself even beer'.

Kvass is a very early Slavonic drink. It is mentioned in A.D. 100, and is still widely drunk. An old custom at funerals was to hand round a mixture of mead, beer and wine, etc. The mourners stood while the priests recited the final prayers, then all drank to the departed soul. The mixture was called Trisna, after the name of this ancient Slavonian funeral ceremony.

Oldest of all, though not Slavonic, is the Tartar drink called Koumiss. It is so ancient that it is mentioned in Herodotus, and is made from mare's milk. It is still drunk in the Kirghiz region of the U.S.S.R. and is highly nutritious. It is often recommended for invalids, especially consumptives. Traditionally it is made either in smoked horse-skins or in wooden tubs, and an eau de vie can be produced by fermenting it. (The Caucasians also make a drink from fermented camel's milk.)

Ten champagne quart bottles of koumiss are said to supply all the nourishment needed by a strong fully-grown adult.

Wine

The Russians learnt to drink wine from the Greeks through their contact with Byzantium, before the Mongol invasion. Wine-drinking was also closely connected with Christian church ritual. During the Tartar domination, communication was broken with the Eastern Empire and wine was no longer drunk, but the custom was revived in the time of the Tsars. Greek wine was later replaced by Hungarian and finally French wines, introduced by Peter the Great, who also imported vines for growing in the Crimea.

Wine was made in Astrakhan as early as 1613 but though the grapes were excellent the wine was said to have a strange flavour, possibly from the goat skins in which it was kept.

Caucasian and Crimean wines and sherries soon became appreciated by foreigners. The best Soviet wines still come from these areas. Champagne is also made. Though certain Russians reject all drinks but vodka there are many who cannot resist champagne.

This wine, usually associated with the more cosmopolitan aristocracy of Tsarist days, was also appreciated by the nineteenth-century Kalmuck prince who entertained Alexandre Dumas:

'When we reached the dessert stage, the prince asked me to come to the window, glass in hand, to receive a toast from the Kalmucks still feasting outside. As I appeared they all rose to their feet, each with his wooden drinking vessel in one hand and a half-gnawed bone in the other, gave me a cheer and drank my health. The prince decided that my glass was too small for an adequate response, so he handed me a great horn bound with silver, poured into it a whole bottle of champagne, and though I am no drinker I managed to drain it in honour of his subjects, the three hundred in the courtyard and their eleven thousand fellow-serfs throughout his realm.'

Vodka

Russians do not consider a meal complete without vodka, specially for the zakuski course. There is much to be said for the practice. The clean spirit, served icy cold, is the perfect accompaniment to smoked or salted fish, rich mayonnaise and sour cream dishes. It is always drunk neat. It is never sipped; it should be swallowed in one gulp and is served in glasses just big enough to hold this amount. Though it looks innocuous it is potent and quickly warms up the most frigid guest. The custom of drinking neat spirit in cold countries was probably designed for this purpose for it not only thaws out those who have travelled through the snow but breaks the social ice.

Vodka is drunk by women as well as men, though perhaps in smaller quantities. Some Russian restaurants supply free zakuski for their drinkers without loss, since the amount of liquor consumed pays for the food. A pretty custom was for the friends of a newly-engaged man to spell out his fiancée's name in vodka glasses and expect him to empty them all to prove his love.

True vodka, which is made from wheat, is colourless and looks like water; but there are different varieties. (Gogol talks of 'six different vodkas, surrounded by a necklace of zakuski'.) Some of the best known are zubrowka, from Poland, pale almond-green with a faint aromatic scent from the herbs infused in it; vishniowka, cherry vodka, which is red; lemon or orange vodka in which peel is infused; and pepper and strong pepper vodka for those who can take them.

Kvass

Kvass is a drink made from black bread and yeast. It is the great drink of the Russian peasant and is frequently mentioned in Russian literature. It is harmless and is used in cold soups, such as Okroshka. In summer it is sold in restaurants and in the streets from small tanks. It is very slightly alcoholic.

When making kvass put it in the refrigerator as soon as bottled, using corks, not screw-in stoppers. If it is not chilled at once it will go on fermenting and if the seething liquid cannot blow its cork it will shatter the bottle. This once happened in Nina's kitchen.

KVASS

FOR ABOUT TEN BOTTLES

1 *pound dry black bread*
24 *cups boiling water*
1½ *pound sugar*
2 *ounces fresh yeast compressed*
½ *cup sultanas*

Put the bread into a big saucepan or earthenware crock and pour the boiling water over it. Allow it to cool until lukewarm, then carefully squeeze the liquid from the bread, straining through a muslin cloth so that no bread comes through, which would cloud the kvass. Add the sugar and yeast. Mix, cover and leave for 10–12 hours.

Pour the kvass into clean bottles, add 2 or 3 sultanas to each, cork and tie down. Put into the refrigerator *immediately* and keep there until needed.

This is the normal kvass, but there are other drinks which might be regarded as variations — Yablochinkvas (Cider); Grusheviikvas (Perry — made from pears); Malinovoi, from raspberries.

Fruit-wine Liqueurs

Some of the Russian women make very pleasant home-made liqueurs, from mulberries, raspberries, loganberries, cherries, etc., and though perhaps sometimes they are inclined to be rather sweet, the best make a good accompaniment to black coffee.

Half fill a ½ gallon bottle or jar with berries; add sugar till the jar is full. Cover and leave to ferment, for 6–8 weeks. The berries should settle down into the juice so that no bubbles remain.

Put the berries through a fine sieve, squeezing out the juice. Filter everything through a thin layer of cotton wool or a very fine cloth. The juice should be quite clear. Add alcohol to the strength you wish, using vodka, brandy or cognac. The easiest way to filter is to put a funnel into the neck of the bottle, lay cotton-wool in it and pour the liquid through from the fermenting-jar.

Cruchons and Punches

In Georgia, where some of the best U.S.S.R. red and white wines are made and drunk, Cruchon is a popular summer drink. It is really a delicate fruit punch.

CAUCASIAN FRUIT PUNCH
(*Kavkaski Cruchon*)

FOR ABOUT 2 PINTS

1 *pound fruit — peaches, apricots, cherries, pineapple, etc.*
1 *bottle sweet white wine*
1 *liqueur-glass cognac*
sliced peel from ¼ lemon
sliced rind of ½ cucumber

Cut up the fruit, removing stones, and half fill a large glass jug. Mix together the rest of the ingredients and pour over. Chill thoroughly. Drink the punch and eat the fruit afterwards.

FANTASY FRUIT PUNCH
(*Fantasia Cruchon*)
FOR ABOUT 4 PINTS

1 pound any fruit in season
1 bottle white port
1 bottle madeira
wine-glass cognac
sugar to taste — the quantity depends on whether fruit is sweet or not
juice of half a lemon

Chop up the fruit. Mix together other ingredients and pour over. Leave for at least half an hour, preferably longer, in the refrigerator, and drink very cold.

HOT PUNCH
(*Goryachi Punsh*)
FOR ONE PERSON

1 wine-glass brandy
1 ounce icing sugar
dash of lemon juice
¼ pint boiling water

Mix all ingredients together and drink hot. This quantity makes punch for *one person*, so should be multiplied according to number of servings needed.

HOT MILK PUNCH
(*Molachni Punsh, Goryachi*)
FOR ONE PERSON

1 liqueur-glass brandy or any chosen liqueur
¼ ounce icing sugar
¼ pint milk
nutmeg

Put brandy and sugar into a glass. Boil the milk and pour over while hot. Dust with nutmeg. Both these punches would be improved by using cognac instead of brandy.

Russian Tea (Russki Chai)

Like vodka and kvass, tea is one of Russia's national beverages and few homes are without a samovar or tea urn. These are also found in public tea rooms, tea gardens, even cemeteries.

Because of their trade and contact with China, the people in the east of Russia early became used to the highest quality Chinese tea. They drank brick tea, and yellow tea which is pale and has a delicious flavour, though said to be bad for the nerves. Yellow tea, which is taken after dinner instead of coffee, was much preferred to brick tea, which is made from tea-leaves that have been steamed, crushed in a mortar and made into cakes.

To the Russians, the samovar is more than a tea urn; it is a symbol of hospitality and family life. Tolstoy calls it a 'sacred shrine'. In big households, dispensing tea was quite a ritual.

Though many modern samovars are wired for electricity, the traditional model is heated with charcoal, contained in a central cylinder. The tea is made in a pot and stood on top of the samovar and the hot water singing inside is drawn off through a little tap. About half an inch of very strong tea is poured into the cup or glass — men drink tea from glasses, women from cups — and the rest filled with hot water. It is usually drunk with lemon, but some people drink it with honey, cream or milk or put a spoonful of jam — raspberry, blackberry, blackcurrant — into the tea and a few slices of apple on top. In Russian jam the fruit is left intact, not mashed up, because it is not intended for spreading on bread. It is eaten with a teaspoon from a little saucer.

This custom of adding fruit, jam, etc., is a relic of an ancient Chinese practice which the Russians learnt from the Chinese merchants. The tea was boiled with rice, ginger, salt, orange-peel, spices, milk and sometimes onions. Some Tibetan, Nepalese and Mongolian tribes still make a similar syrup; and the Kalmucks and Kirghiz of the Steppes think highly of brick tea, as poor Dumas discovered: '. . . an abominable beverage . . . made from a piece of tea-brick from China, boiled in a saucepan with milk, butter and salt.'

Typical Russian Menus

BREAKFAST

Omelette with Sour Cream Sauce
Cream Cheese Spread with Caraway Seeds
Toast
Tea or Coffee

Scrambled Egg with Frankfurters
Yoghurt
Toast
Tea or Coffee

Breakfast Semolina
Sweet Cream Cheese
Toast
Tea or Coffee

LUNCH

Noodles, Sailor Style
Pumpkin Pudding

Pilaff with Eggs and Ham
Sweet Cream Cheese Paste

Crab and Rice Croquettes
Baked Fish with Egg

Fried Pancake Pies
Hvorost

DINNER

Zakuski
Fish Soup
Fish Kotlet with Mushroom Sauce
Cream Cheese Patties

Zakuski
Fish Soup with Salted Cucumber
Fish Gratin
Apple Charlotte with Egg Sauce

Zakuski
Moscow Borsch
Pork Fillets with Apples
Kisel

Zakuski
Kidney and Cucumber Soup
Chicken Fillets in Breadcrumbs
Pancake Pies with Cream Cheese

Zakuski
Georgian Soup
Chahohbili of Chicken
Rice Pudding with Kisel

Zakuski
Okroshka with Crab Meat
Pot Roast in Aspic
Ice Cream — Plombir

SPECIAL DINNERS OR PARTIES

Zakuski: Salted Herring; Hot-smoked Fish; Smoked Salmon; Grilled Half-eggs; Stuffed Green Peppers; Liver Paste; Egg with Horseradish.

Soup

Cabbage Soup served with
Deep-fried Little Pies with Cabbage Filling

Meat

Ham Cooked in Beer

Dessert

Coffee Parfait
Sweet Cakes with Coffee

Zakuski: Crab with Mayonnaise; Anchovies on Eggs; Fish in Aspic; Marinaded Fish in Tomato Sauce; Potato Salad; Fresh Spring Salad; Radishes in Sour Cream.

Soup

Spring Soup served with Little Pies with
Spring Onion and Egg Filling

Meat

Roast Duck with Apples

Dessert

Fruit Surprise
Tort à la Madame Pavlova, with Coffee

Supplies for Russian Cooking

A Russian housewife usually has in her store-cupboard or refrigerator some or all of the following, for everyday meals:

EVERYDAY SUPPLIES

kasha (buckwheat)
flour
sunflower or peanut oil
black bread
rye bread
noodles
rice
peppercorns
cloves
cinnamon
mustard
paprika
sugar
castor sugar
icing sugar
honey
jams
horseradish — bought or home-made
dried mushrooms
acetic acid (used instead of vinegar)

TINNED FOODS

anchovies
sprats
sardines

kilkies (Norwegian anchovies)
caviar — red or black (*must* be kept in the refrigerator)
tinned soups
tomato purée
tinned mushrooms
asparagus

DAIRY FOODS

sour cream — bought or home-made
yoghurt ,, ,, ,,
cheeses
cream cheese
eggs

PRESERVED FOODS

marinated fruits and vegetables
pickled cucumbers
dried fruits and peel
salted herring
smoked and boiled ham

Meat and more perishable smoked fish are bought as needed. The fresh vegetables most frequently used are:
cabbage
potatoes
mushrooms
onions
shallots or spring onions
vegetable marrows
green and red peppers
tomatoes
cucumber
aubergine
carrots
beetroot

The most popular herbs and flavourings are garlic, dill, parsley, bay leaves, chives. If dill is not available, substitute parsley, though this is a second-best.

Busy working wives probably keep ready-made deep-frozen pelemeni in the freezer and for unexpected visitors tinned or frozen delicacies such as crab, Boeuf Stroganoff, etc.

Cooking Equipment

No special kitchen implements are needed. A set of skewers with wooden handles, such as sold for barbecues, will do for shaslik; a deep rather than wide pot, very big indeed, is best for making borsch, and you want some good sharp knives for filleting fish and chicken. Use large coffee or dried-milk tins instead of the special mould for baba or kulich, and use a colander or flower-pot instead of the special wooden paskha mould.

Other necessary items are a pan for deep-frying; a good-sized pan for making blini (Russian pancakes); a saucepan big enough to boil pelemeni and a perforated spoon for lifting them out.

In the old days most of the cooking pots were of cast iron, with a few copper utensils, and wooden bowls and spoons were used. The typical Russian stove — Russkaya Piechka — was enormous, built into the wall with a hot plate — plita — in front, a baker's oven behind it and quite often a shelf above it where the servants, the very old or the very young liked to lie to keep warm.

FOR THE TABLE

For Russian meals, everyone should have two plates, one slightly smaller than the other, and two forks. Plenty of small dishes for zakuski are essential. It is a good idea to collect serving dishes, platters and tureens of all kinds including old-fashioned compôtes which are useful for torts and cakes and marinated fruits. Little forks of silver or mother of pearl are good for helping yourself to zakuski. Vodka glasses are an important item. They should be 1-ounce size, just big enough for one gulp.

For tea, a samovar is of course traditional, but émigrés who no longer possess one manage quite well without. For daily use, a modern samovar, wired for electricity, is the most practical.

The Metric System

WEIGHT

1 oz — 28.35 g	1 kilogramme —	1000 g —	2 lb 3 oz	approx.
2 oz — 56.7 g		500 g —	1 lb 1½ oz	„
¼ lb — 113.4 g		250 g —	9 oz	„
½ lb — 226.8 g		125 g —	4¼ oz	„
12 oz — 340.2 g		100 g —	3½ oz	„
16 oz — 453.6 g		25 g —	1 oz	„

LIQUIDS

¼ pt (1 gill) — 142 ml
½ pt — 284 ml
1 pt — 568 ml

1 litre	— 1000 g	— 1¾ pt — 35 fl oz	approx.
½ litre	— 500 g	— ¾ pt plus 4½ tablespoons	„
¼ litre	— 250 g	— ½ pt less 2 tablespoons	„
1 decilitre	— 100 g	— 6 tablespoons	„
1 centilitre	— 10 g	— 1 dessertspoon	„
1 millilitre	— 1 g	— a few drops	„
5 millilitres	— 5 g	— pharmaceutical teaspoon	„

Temperatures

ELECTRICITY AND SOLID FUEL

	Gas	° Fahrenheit	° Centigrade
Cool	¼–½	250	121
Very slow	1	275	135
Slow	2	300	149
	3	325	163
Moderate	4	350	177
	5	375	190
Moderately hot	6	400	205
Hot	7	425	218
Very hot	8	450	232
	9	475	246

Index